THE
SULLIVAN FAMILY
Fifty Years In Bluegrass Gospel Music
1949 - 1999

by
Enoch and Margie Sullivan

with
Robert Gentry

edited by
Patricia Martinez

Published by
Sweet Dreams Publishing Company
P. O. Box 850 ~ Many, La. 71449
Ph. (318) 256-3495 FAX (318) 256-9151
PRINTED IN THE UNITED STATES OF AMERICA

Contents

Foreword

It was a starlit night some 48 years ago when I first heard Brother Enoch and Sister Margie Sullivan play and sing.

They were holding services at our neighbor's house in the backwoods of Washington County in Southwest Alabama. The porch was filled with friends and neighbors. I was a young, barefoot girl sitting at their feet drinking in every word!

I was transported to the stars and beyond when Sister Margie sang "Crooked Street to Glory Avenue." I remember the words, "No mortgage on my property; and the rent it don't come due. I see you are in an awful fix; I'll tell you what to do. Just move right off of Crooked Street to Glory Avenue."

Recently the Sullivans "came home" to a little country church near St. Stephens, AL, and their home and old stomping grounds. The church is in Frankville, AL and it is here they made some of their very first public appearances as country, bluegrass gospel singers and players.

The old home they first played in is gone. The couple who lived there, Mr. Needman and Mrs. Jennie Henson, have also gone on to Glory. Many of our neighbors, friends and family have gone home. The little country church beckoned like a lighthouse; yes, the Sullivans were home.

Their voices blended as they sang, "Swing Low Sweet Chariot." The chariot seems to swing so low I wanted to get on board and go see my son. I could almost feel the chariot taking flight. I know they can sing like that because their son is waiting with mine just inside the gates of heaven.

Brother Enoch and Sister Margie are proud of their old home place where their roots were first anchored in the Lord.

When the service was over, they came to me. As my mind wandered, I was a barefoot girl again sitting at their feet. They asked me to write the foreword in this book. I swallowed and stood there speechless! They could have asked anyone of dozens of people of fame and fortune—but they asked me. That's the Sullivans, their music and their book glorifies one name - the Lord Jesus Christ.

Come on in, meet and get to know Sister Margie and Brother Enoch Sullivan. Sit on the porch and sing along with homefolks.

Frances Richardson
Frankville, AL
March 20, 1999

An Introduction

If you're a fan of bluegrass music, and almost everyone is, then somewhere along the line you have seen or heard the Sullivan Family of St. Stephens, AL. The year 1999 marks their 50th Anniversary in the bluegrass gospel music field.

Music was a big part of the early lives of Enoch Sullivan and Margie Brewster early on.

Enoch's father, the Rev. Arthur Sullivan, played string band music back in the 1930's and 40's. They patterned their music very much like Wade Mainer and the Mainer's Mountaineers.

And over in Winnsboro, LA, Margie Louise Brewster loved country and old-time music. She loved Molly O'Day, Kitty Wells and Martha Carson. Her father purchased a guitar for her at an early age and the mold was cast. She left home at 13 to be the singer and guitarist for an evangelist named Hazel Chain.

Her work was more than a job for her. It was also a ministry. And it has remained so all these many years. It was through this ministry that she and Sister Chain went to Alabama where she met her future husband.

Earlier something happened to Brother Arthur that would forever change his life and that of his family. They had been playing what they called "frolic" music at dances in the southwest Alabama area. Brother Arthur had a near-death illness and when he recovered, he devoted the rest of his life to preaching, praying and singing the old-fashion way.

Both Enoch and Margie now look back and say

1

their meeting was love at first sight. They were married December 16, 1949 and later that month with Brother Arthur started their first radio program on WRJW in Picayune, MS. That was the beginning of the Sullivan family.

This was the beginning of their professional career and they have stuck with it through thick and thin for 50 years.

In early 1950, Emmett Sullivan, Enoch's brother joined the group playing banjo and he remained an intricate and important part until his death.

Brother Arthur was in church one night and had finished his sermon. He turned from the pulpit, humbly knelt at an altar, had a heart attack and died. If he could have had a choice about his death, he wouldn't have done it any differently.

His death left a big void in the Sullivan Family and for awhile Enoch and Margie wondered about whether they should continue the work. They thought about it. They prayed about it. They had a radio broadcast scheduled the following Sunday and had to make a decision.

Enoch took the bull by the horns and said, "We're gonna do it." And they did. It was the right decision and has led them across the world with their music and their work for the Lord.

They have recorded, played concerts in almost all states and many foreign countries and made television appearances. They were voted into Bill Monroe's Bluegrass Hall of Fame. They have appeared on the world-famous Grand Ole Opry. They've played for governors, congressmen and others of prominence. They have worked in the smallest churches and in the largest. They've played with some of the top stars in the fields of country, bluegrass and gospel.

The Sullivans will tell you right off that their hero is the late-great Father of Bluegrass Music Bill Monroe. They are proud of the help they feel Mr. Monroe gave them through the years. Even now, they speak of Mr. Monroe with reverence, with dignity and with honor. But you'll read in this book that maybe the Sullivans had a lot to do with helping Mr. Monroe back in the days when rock and roll had almost choked country and bluegrass music.

It's true, the Sullivans were playing bluegrass gospel music before it even had a name. They called it "string band music" early on. It was Mr. Monroe who named the music years later after his band "The Bluegrass Boys," which had been named for his native state of Kentucky, the Bluegrass State.

And it was Mr. Monroe, sometime later, who named the Sullivan's music "Bluegrass Gospel." Enoch and Margie are very proud of that distinction and very proud that the head man decided to give it that name.

The Sullivan's music is emotional. It carries a message. It tells a story. It comes from the heart. It always has and it always will.

I think you will enjoy reading about the happy times, the trials and the tribulations and the music and work of this "First Family of Bluegrass Gospel Music."

Robert Gentry
Many, La.
April 21, 1999

Chapter 1

Enoch Sullivan

We're real proud of our heritage. Our forefathers were honorable men and we feel real proud that they stood for what they thought was right and stood for it firmly until their death. They were that way in business and anything else. They were honest people. We always tried to pattern our lives along that same line. If we told someone something that we were going to do, we tried to stick with it.

I was born September 18, 1931 in Washington County, AL about four miles south of St. Stephens, between there and Wagarville, AL. My dad was Arthur Sullivan and my mother was Florence Bailey Sullivan. My grandparents on my daddy's side were James Buchanan Sullivan and his wife, Hattie Aseline Knapp Sullivan. My great-grandparents on this side were Jim and Alice Sullivan. Going back farther, my great, great grandfather was Gibeon Sullivan, who fought for the Confederacy.

My grandparents on my mother's side were John Gibeon Bailey and Ann Melissa Mosley Bailey. Also, my great grandfather on my mother's side was Elij Bailey, who was in the same company as Gib Sullivan. He too was captured at the Battle of Nashville. The Bailey side of the family goes on back to Tom Walker Bailey, my great, great-grandfather. He operated a tanning factory near St. Stephens in the early years. That's just a little bit of the history.

My first recollection was right there at my birthplace. Both St. Stephens and Wagarville had little Baptist Churches. My forebearers were members of the Baptist Church. Since we lived half way between the two little towns, we didn't have a church in our community. Back then, church was sometime held just once a month. My parents failed to take a very big part in church. In fact, I can't remember them going to church with me until I was somewhere around seven or eight years old.

My dad was stricken with a heart attack and went into a coma. We thought he was going to die. People came from far and near around the community to pray for him. After the second day, he regained consciousness and wanted something to eat. I remember very plain that just as soon as he got able to speak, he wanted to talk to my Mother. He called her to the bed and told her that our lives and our home would be different. He said he was going to church. He said if the Lord was kind enough to raise him up and make him able to go to church, then he was going and he would take his family with him.

The Lord saw fit to let him live and he did just what he said. He started taking us to church. Right there is where I became acquainted with a very strong religious upbringing. It was very primitive. As I say, we didn't have a church to go to. So Dad said right away, "Well, we'll just build a brush arbor." It was a place where we could have church; close enough so we could walk to it. Sometime we would ride on a little ole two-wheel oxen cart, or a mule wagon or sometime just walk. Kids love to walk and we'd go to church. That made a big difference in our lives, right there.

It was at church that I got introduced to music. I knew I loved music, but up until the time Dad was converted, I'd heard what was called "frolic music." The family would get together and my grandfather, J. B. Sullivan, could play the banjo real good and somebody would play the fiddle and so they would play the music. The people would dance and have just a good home "frolic," they called it. I knew I loved that kind of music.

6

When we got a "talkin' machine," or victrola my Grandfather Bailey told me that I needed to get the music of Gid Tanner, Riley Puckett, Clayton McMichen and "Fiddlin" Arthur Smith. I learned in later years they were all part of a group called the "Georgia Wildcats," who worked out of Atlanta, GA. and were very popular musicians. They didn't travel much and we didn't get to see them, but they were a great influence on my life. I knew I liked that kind of music and so that's the kind of records we bought. I played them and listened very closely and I started taking an interest in the music from that. Riley Puckett was a good guitar player. I think all guitar players from that period, including Lester Flatt, Charlie Monroe and others, patterned their music a little bit after Riley Puckett.

The first band I heard play the sounds of bluegrass music was actually Mainer's Mountaineers out of North Carolina. They had a band that featured all five of the main instruments, guitar, fiddle, banjo, mandolin and bass. I loved that music very much and I would listen to their recordings. Some of those records I've been talking about were probably recorded in 1928 and '29. That was the first music that interested me.

When Dad was converted, he changed that. He didn't believe in the kind of music I was listening to and he wanted us to play all church music. I went to church and I learned a lot. I first learned on the guitar playing in the church choir. It was a string band choir, not a fashionable choir, just community people gathered together singing from an old songbook. I learned to play the guitar at about eight and then started playing the mandolin about a year later at nine and the fiddle at about 10-years-old.

Our family went to church devoutly and on a

regular basis. We'd go on Sunday to Sunday school and worship and then on Sunday night. You couldn't come up with an excuse that could keep you from going to church. I know I tried lots of different things to start with. I tried playing sick, but if you were sick, then they'd put you through the prayer line and that was embarrassing to a young fellow. I soon learned that you couldn't get by with playing sick. If you didn't die, you had to go. If you wanted to go rabbit hunting, you'd try to figure a way to get out of going to church, but there was no use. Dad wouldn't let you do it.

As kids we liked to go swimming. We had a placed called "Sullivan's Lake," where I spent many good, happy hours of my life. In the summertime, the heat in the South can get pretty hot. We did what was called "pea-patch farming," which was just small patches of peas, corn and mostly stuff for us to eat and also for the animals. When we'd be working in the fields and get real hot, we'd take off for the swimming hole. If you were lucky enough to have a watermelon to carry down there with you, you'd eat watermelon and enjoy that, too.

We loved to hunt and that was always an important part of our lives. We had lots of land to hunt on, it being rural Alabama, and you didn't need a permit. We loved to hunt for squirrel and rabbit. I always had a good rabbit dog. I also loved to deer hunt and had good dogs. People gathered at our house for years, even after I grew up and we'd go hunting.

Speaking of getting out of church, I remember an incident that happened which is funny now, but it wasn't so funny when it happened. My younger brother Emmett was easily persuaded as a little boy. I had an uncle, Homer Lee Sullivan, who lived in Mobile and he would come up on weekends and he liked to hunt. My uncle and Emmett got together and figured out a way for Emmett to get out of going to church.

Emmett played sick and the rest of us went on to Sunday school and church.

Emmett, Uncle Homer Lee and my old rabbit dog "Queen" decided to go on a little hunt while we were having Sunday school. Right half way through the service at the little church, we heard someone screaming. I mean, just hollering and screaming with every breath. We ran outside the church to see what it was and there was Emmett. He was just a young fellow and he was screaming to the top of his voice and he was scared to death. I made a mad dash to get to him. I figured something was wrong and when I got to him he told me he had shot Uncle Homer Lee.

I said, "Where is he?"

"He's back over these hills," Emmett told me and I said, "Let's go."

We ran as hard as we could to get there. When we got there, Uncle Homer Lee was half scared to death. We knew that when an animal was wounded it went to water to stop the bleeding. He thought he was bleeding to death, so he pulled himself down to a little stream of water to stop the blood. When I asked him where he was shot, he replied, "Well, I'm shot right in the rear."

"How in the world did it happen?" I asked.

He replied, "Well, we were running. The dog was running the rabbit and we were running after the dog and I was in front. Emmett was running behind me with his gun loaded and he fell down. When he did, the barrel of his gun went into the mud, the hammer of the gun hit an little ole piece of wood and the gun went off."

The whole load of shot went into my uncle's rear.

9

He thought he was dying and so he would hardly help himself at all.

He said, "Oh son, I'm dying. I'm dying, son. I'm dying."

We got him on our shoulders the best we could because we had to get him out of the woods and to a car. We finally got him to a car and carried him to the doctor.

When the doctor undressed him, you know he had to pull all his clothes off, well, he told him, "You just turn over, and stoop over here and let me see where you're shot before we can do anything for you."

So the doctor examined him. He found that the whole load of shot, which was rabbit shot, and therefore not very big (and by the gun being stopped up the shot didn't have full power) had gone right into my uncle's rear just under the skin.

My uncle wanted to know if he was going to die and the doctor told him, "Mr. Sullivan, you're not exactly dangerously shot, you're just painfully shot." We all had a big laugh and he got over it and was all right after that. He's still a wonderful fellow and he loves the music, but he never tried to rabbit hunt on Sunday any more. Nor did Emmett; that stopped it right there.

I started school at seven; my birthday came in a way that they didn't send me the first year. We had to walk about two miles to catch the school bus. It was kind of hard to do it in the wintertime. I didn't go to school very much the first year, but I did manage to go enough to pass to the second grade.

I never did love school because I loved the outdoors so well. It seemed to me that school was kind of like a prison. I couldn't go on and do the things that I wanted to do. They had prayer in the mornings and Bible readings. It was a lot like church. I enjoyed it and the teacher not only taught us from our books, but she taught us right from wrong and assisted in what our parents taught us, too. We were taught to be honest and fair, to treat our fellowman right, to fear God and to believe in God and country. I'm still a strong believer in that. I don't see how in the world you can be successful in a home or in marriage, in raising a family or in business, politics or anything else without acknowledging fear in God and having prayer and putting your faith in Jesus Christ. Sometime life is bad enough anyway, but if you take that away, then you can't hope for anything but more trouble.

The games we played were seesaw and swings, but my main pleasure was ball. I loved baseball and football. Marbles was a wonderful game that I enjoyed. I had some buddies that I'll never forget because they were like family to me and I saw them everyday. Edward Hendricks, a fine Christian-hearted boy, was my best friend. There was also Jimmy Glover, Gene Blunt and Gaines and Matt Granade and the Ethridges, a great family of good people. We had the best time. Edward, Gene and Jimmy and me played as partners in marbles. We could play pretty good and we got to where we had a pretty good stack of marbles. We thought we were doing all right, but Dad found out about me having all those marbles.

"Where did you get 'em?" he asked. I replied, "We played marbles at school."

"You played for keeps?" he asked, and I answered, "Yes, sir."

Dad said, "Well don't you know that's wrong.

You're gambling and you shouldn't be doing that. That's their marbles and I don't want you doing that no more-don't play for keeps. You can't keep their marbles. You can keep 'em until the game is over, but then you give 'em back."

I found out right then and there that gambling is wrong and so I figured there was no use to gamble if you couldn't keep the marbles anyhow, so I just quit gambling. We'd just have a game and when the game was over, everybody got his marbles back and we'd start over again. We had just as much fun and everybody still had the same amount of marbles, too. That was mainly what school consisted of back in those days. We didn't travel too much from one school to another playing ball or anything like that.

I always loved animals. I loved horses and stock and enjoyed tending them with my granddaddy Bailey and granddaddy Sullivan. Both my granddaddies were fine teamsters. They could drive and train stock really good, both mules and oxen. That was their profession. They worked for different logging companies as mule and oxen drivers.

On the farm we had some calves from the milk cows. I'd have a little yoke fixed up and I'd train them to be used on the farm. I loved to train the animals. I also loved to train the horses and I loved to ride them. I love pretty animals.

I remember when Emmett was born. It was at home, you know, you didn't go to the hospital back then. We had what we called a midwife, or in this case the doctor came to the house. Dr. Herbert Peters lived about three miles from our house and came in a Model T Ford and delivered Emmett. And then Joyce, my oldest sister, was born at home, too. I remember that the midwife came. She was an old colored lady named Charlotte Savage. She was an old-time colored minister's wife. And then Jewel was born at home with the same Aunt Charlotte, which is what we called her. She was a wonderful, wonderful person. Then my next sister, Norma, was born in the hospital and so were the rest of the kids.

I was born at home too and the midwife that was there was also a colored lady named Aunt Jane Fettaway. I won't ever forget the Fettaways were friends of our family. There was one other interesting thing that always fascinated me. I was born at Granddaddy Bailey's house. My mother and my daddy and I were all born in the same house, in the same room and on the same bed. My granddaddy was my daddy's great uncle and his mother (my grandmother) came to be there when she had my daddy.

After Dad's heart attack he was never able to do any manual labor, but he was able to go to church. We went on and did the best we could farming and just making ends meet. The grandparents on both sides, the Sullivans and Baileys, helped as much as they could.

I went to school until I was about 14 years old, I think. I believe it was about the eighth grade. Then Dad worsened, it seemed. He had another round with his heart and the family was getting larger all the time; my brothers and sisters were coming on. There had to be somebody to go to work. My grandfather Sullivan was doing some logging contracting and he told my dad, "If you'll let the boy come and work, we'll make it, don't worry. I'll let the boy go to work out there in the log woods with me and that'll help and whatever we have, we'll have it together." And that's what we did. I learned all the trades of logging at that particular time, like saw filing, driving the trucks, driving the mule and oxen teams and I learned to cut timber with a cross-cut saw. It was hard work, but I enjoyed it and that was what I wanted to do. What money we made, we brought to the house and my grandfather divided it and we made our living in this way. Everybody was in the same boat.

I remember going to the picture show. You'd really want to go, even thought it cost a dime to get in. You had to pay a quarter to ride the bus to the theater. That was a total of 35 cents and it was hard, so we didn't go much because we just didn't have the money to spare. As I said, my dad was a minister and he was very strict and he didn't exactly like for us to go to the movies. He thought it was worldly and I can see his point. He didn't want us to get into things we didn't have any business in and he didn't want us influenced by the wrong things.

Back in those days the picture shows were wholesome. There was mostly Gene Autry and Roy Rogers and it was a lot of fun. I can remember Johnny Mack Brown and Lash LaRue and all of them. That was way back and I enjoyed them when I could go.

There's a funny story about all of it. My dad was a real sick man with a family and the times were hard and he worried about how we would survive. In those days most men worried a lot. In my family, we always tried to keep it from the ladies. We figured they had enough on their hands raising a family anyhow and we didn't want to bother my grandmothers and my mother. The men wouldn't talk about it being hopeless in front of them.

One day I remember Dad was feeling so bad and pressed with the bills and trying to raise the family and he said, "Let's go to Papas and talk to him." That was my Grandfather J. B.; my daddy called him "Papa" and I called him "Papa," too.

So we walked down to my grandparent's house. They didn't have an elaborate house, just a little ole cottage. It was just a little frame house. They had a livingroom with a fireplace and two beds. It was a livingroom and a bedroom too for my grandparents. They had a chimney, made of mud and sticks. When it rained, it washed down. Anyhow, that was the type chimney and they were warming in there by the fire, as it was cool weather. The kitchen was off from the house. It was a log kitchen and it had a walkway to it. My grandmother cooked on a wood stove and they ate in that room.

We talked family talk in the living room by the fire for awhile and then we started to leave. My family has a way, and still has that way; they'll walk up the road a short distance with you when you start to go home. My daddy bid my grandmother good-bye and then Papa decided he was going up the road with us and we'd talk. We finally got to a place where he stopped. The road had a bank and we sat down there.

My grandfather smoked. He smoked all his life. I'll never forget, his hands were green from the nicotine because he smoked the cigarettes down so short. He rolled a cigarette and he used brown paper, you know, because he didn't have cigarette papers, not factory made, he just used an old paper sack. He rolled his cigarette and he was talking to Dad.

Dad figured it was time to tell him the bad news and he said, "You know Papa, I don't know what I'm going to do. Florence (speaking of my mother) is up yonder at the house with all them kids. He really called them 'young 'uns.' I ain't got no job and I don't know what in the world I'm gonna do. It looks like we're even running out of anything to eat. I don't know what we're going to do. Sometimes I get so depressed and just down and out that I feel like I ought to end it all-just blow my brains out."

My grandfather was a very devout man and he

15

didn't believe in that. He said, "Oh no, my God son, don't talk like that. Yes, I know it looks bad."

I noticed by Grandfather was rolling that cigarette. He'd go t it ready and was about to light it. He looked right at my daddy. He was real blue-eyed and I could tell he was fixing to pull some kind of a little joke. His eyes were bright looking and cunning, they were twinkling and he said, "No son, just think about it like this. Say take me and your mother. Now you look at us. We started out with practically nothing and just look at what we got now."

It broke my daddy up and he started laughing, then we all laughed until we cried. Daddy said, "Yes sir, that's what I'm looking at Papa. I see what you got and it's been 50 years of it and you still ain't got nothing."

Papa replied, "Well, don't think about them bad things." So we parted and went back to the house and it seemed like everything was all right. That's all it took, right then. Papa always had a way of making you feel better about it all at the very worst times you could have.

I had been to school a little, and it seemed to me that the job we were working on cutting timber had us loosing money every day. I figured on it some and one day me and Papa were eating lunch under a shade tree and I told him, "Papa, we might as well quit and go to the house. We ain't doing no good; we're going in the hole. Every day we're loosing money."

"Oh no son, we can't do that," he said, "we can't go to the house, we gotta work. That don't make no difference about goin' in the hole. We gotta work anyhow. Them women won't let us come home, so we might as well work."

He was real comical and he was a good man. He taught me how to work the first day I was with him. You don't ever forget that. He was patient with me and he told me the best ways to do it. He was honest and he believed in treating people right. He believed that even if sometime it was at your expense to do so; you kept your word. I won't ever forget either of my grandparents. They were strict in that way.

I saw my grandfather Bailey do one of the most honest things I ever saw. I know it was honest because he had an option to do it either way. He had homesteaded some land he lived on and had bargained to buy it from the company. His cousin worked for that company and they sent him over to my grandfather's in the later years of his life. He told my grandfather, "I come Gib to give you a chance if you want this land to sign these papers. It makes it legal, you give me $1.00 and sign and it's yours because you've been here long enough. It's yours by homestead."

"Well, I ain't got a dollar," my grandfather replied. His cousin said, "Well, I got a dollar. I brought a dollar."

My grandfather studied him a minute and said, "No, I can't do that anyhow, 'cause I bargained with the company to buy this land and I didn't get to hold up my end of the bargain. I didn't get to pay for it like I said. And for me to take a dollar from you and give it back to you and sign these papers that I paid for it would be dishonest in my sight, so I can't do that."

The cousin told him, "If you sign now, you're signing away your right to it. My grandfather replied, "Well, that's what I'd rather do. I'm old now anyway and I'd rather do it that way, 'cause I didn't do what I said I'd do."

I saw my grandfather sign the land back to the

company. He was not forced to. His cousin urged him to do it the other way, but he said he'd rather not. He was very honest and there's nothing wrong with that; it's the way life should be. All of us have ups and downs and we have some goals we reach and others we never reach. Just because you don't reach your goal doesn't mean you should turn bad in order to try to do what you think you just want to do. Do right as you go though life.

I think music at an early age played a big part in changing our lives. We leaned heavily on our musical upbringing and we met so many good friends and so many good things happened to us through the music.

From about the time I was 10 in 1941, we went to church and people came by and picked us up and carried us to church. Sometime we'd walk to church and stay overnight at a friend's house, play the music and go to church. I remember the first trip I ever made out of Washington County, to Clark County, which is just across the river, about 12-14 miles. I had a friend that had a 1938 Chevrolet, a pretty new car, and he took us. We went there and then the next time we went out of the county was when we went to Enterprise, AL. I believe that was to Coffee County, about 150 miles from our house. My dad and I went over there. He played the guitar and I played the mandolin and we'd swap back and forth on the instruments. We went to church and I remember meeting friends there that are friends to me yet, after all these years.

People came by and got us to play for homecomings and tent revivals. I remember one time the people in my county were awful good to us. The Beeches, Brother Roy Beech and his brother would send a car after us to help them in their church work. The brother, Ellis, is down in Florida and is still my friend. I remember Devaton Roberts came and got us and the Deerman family in Washington County were

18

close friends to us.

Uncle Will Stoker and his family, they were descendants from people in Virginia and West Virginia, and they could sing so pretty and lonesome. They had a special way of singing that I loved so much. We used to go to their place on an oxen cart to have family prayer meetings. Just the families of the neighbors right around close by. We'd get together and play and sing and pray and maybe someone would preach and testify and we had the best time. I would like to say that those people like the Stokers, Beeches, Roberts and Howards and the people of Washington County were so good to us and I love them so much. It meant so much to get to visit and become friends with them. If we didn't play music, we probably wouldn't have met them. They loved to hear us play and they would come and get us. They would go to a lot of trouble to be with us and we'd just have the best time. And I can't forget Uncle Lonnie Padgett, where I got my first fiddle.

There's a story about the first fiddle that I got. Eli (Buck) Stoker came down to visit us and brought an old fiddle with him. It was a pretty good old fiddle and I loved to play. I'd play Uncle Bud Hiram Lane's fiddle and he was very instrumental in me playing fiddle. Anyway, Mr. Stoker came down and we ate dinner and then we were going to play a little music. He walked out back of the house and saw my dad had a little ole pig. We had a little hog, you know, a little pig that we had in the pen to fatten and kill. When he came back to the house, he said, "Son, you don't have a fiddle?" I replied, "No, sir."

"Why don't you talk to your daddy," he continued. "I noticed you got a pretty little pig down there in the pen. I'll trade you this fiddle for that pig."

I thought, "Man, that's what I want to do." I didn't know how Daddy would take it, but I got to him right quick and told him. I said, "Buck told me that he'd trade me this fiddle for that pig down there. What do you think about it?"

"I don't know," he answered. "I reckon that'd be all right." So we traded. I used that fiddle to play at church. I'd play at the church at Wagarville and that's where I met Uncle Bud Lane, who was a good fiddler. He was as good as there was on the Grand Ole Opry, or anywhere else. He could play lonesome - that's where I learned to play *Rest In The Homeland* from Uncle Bud. He was a renowned fiddler, but didn't travel extensively out on the road. He was an inspiration to me and he helped me learn a lot. Uncle Bud's uncle was Uncle Lonnie Padgett.

The Padgetts were close friends of the Sullivans. Later on as I learned more music, there were more times that I spent with the Padgetts. Hue Gilmer Padgett and his sisters, Josephine, Naomi and Imogene, all played music and we played together with Alpin Sullivan's daughter, Dorothy, who lived in Mobile. She would come up and play the accordion. We played stringed music - guitars and fiddles. I'd play twin fiddle with the accordion. Those were years of good fun and music and friendships and meeting Uncle Lonnie. Uncle Lonnie was Bud Lane's only uncle. I called him uncle too, but he was really not. He was an elderly man and had a real good fiddle that he got from Rayford Lane, Bud's brother who played with Red Stanton's country band out of Meridian, MS. Rayford was a noted fiddler, too.

Uncle Lonnie had traded fiddles with Rayford. It was a real fine fiddle he had ordered from a music company; a brand new one, a good one. I was down at Uncle Lonnie's one evening playing on the porch. He was playing the Lane fiddle and I was playing my 'pig fiddle.' It was easy to tell that his fiddle was much better than mine. We were playing, you know, and I didn't pay too much attention, but he was. We played a tune, I believe it was *Let's Go* or maybe *Wadin' Through Deep Water*, one of the old fiddle tunes. We were playing our fiddles and he looked at me - he was snappy talking, he was Irish a lot - and he said, "Son, I like the way you play that fiddle."

I said, "Well, thank you." He continued, "You need a good fiddle."

"Well, yes sir, I sure do," I told him. He said, "What do you think about us trading fiddles?"

I said, "Well, Uncle Lonnie, my fiddle ain't near the fiddle your fiddle is." I was honest about it, you know. He said, "I understand."

"I couldn't trade because my fiddle is not near as good as yours and I couldn't," I continued. "I wouldn't be able to pay any difference." And he said, "I ain't talking about that. You're a young man and I can tell that you're going to be a good fiddle player in years to come. And any fiddle player needs a good fiddle and I want you to have this one. I'm gonna swap with you 'even' is what I'm talking about."

Even then, I said, "Well, I'll ask Daddy what he thinks about it." So I asked Daddy and he said, "Well son, you know your fiddle is no good."

Daddy told Uncle Lonnie, "That's great, but that old fiddle is not any good." Uncle Lonnie said, "It's good enough for an old man like me." And he took that fiddle and let me have a real good fiddle at a very young age in my life and I still have the fiddle and it's still a good one. But that's the way the first fiddle came about starting out with trading for a pig for one and then just through a friendship I got a real good one.

As time went by, I became a collector of fiddles. I don't pressure people for them, but I love good fiddles and you'd be surprised how many people have given me fiddle, just wanting me to have it as a gift from them.

I remember a dear old preacher friend, John Wesley Dees from Moss Point, MS who was very instrumental in changing my life to always walk the way that I think the Lord would want us to walk. He had a big family and I remember one of his daughters was my girlfriend for awhile; she was a nice, pretty lady. I still love that family very much.

The second brush arbor meeting we had was really with Brother Dees. We went up north from our house to a place called Midway, AL and had a revival meeting under a brush arbor. There was a man converted by the name of George Goldman, and he donated land and built a church. He was a wealthy man and he built the church for the people at Midway. There now stands a beautiful Assembly of God Church at Midway, but it all started with the Sullivans and Brother Dees under that brush arbor.

In that revival, Brother Dees said, "You sure are a good fiddle player and I love to hear you play. I got a fiddle that I want you to have." And he gave it to me. It was foreign made, an Italian fiddle, called "Amati." It had a dragonhead carved on it. I was playing that fiddle in later years at a "tobacco spittin' contest" in Raleigh, MS. The people from the television station in New Orleans, LA were covering it because it was a big international contest. It was a big deal and there were some good spitters there, buddy. Oh man, people from all over came. We had donkey racing, sack racing and all that.

Some of the crew from the television station were going to college and they saw my fiddle. They saw the carving on it and took pictures of it in many different ways, in every way possible. They asked if I'd sign for them to do a class on it at the college down in New Orleans, and they did. People saw my fiddle and would call me about it. I still have it, but I retired it. I don't carry it with me. I was probably about 15-year-old at the time.

Back to the early years at home of hunting and fishing, I'd love to tell you how we used to do. Spring of the year was the time we really looked forward to because we would take off from working the crops or anything that we were doing and go fishing on the Tombigbee River. The river was about three miles on the old wagon roads from our place. We would do "trot line fishing." We'd put out a line all across the Tombigbee River and then we would rake the ponds from crayfish to bait it. There were old crayfish ponds on each side of the river. We'd go there with big five gallon buckets, or whatever, and a crayfish rake and we'd rake the crayfish out and use them to bait the trot lines going across the river.

Then you had one you called "a drop line." You put a big rock on the line and a weight and go half way of the river with that. It would go way down deep to the bottom. We'd go to the river in an oxen cart or mule wagon and we would carry our supplies like corn meal to fry the fish with, the lard and whatever else we needed.

We would take the body off the wagon and lean it against a tree and use it like a lean-to. We put our food under there in case of rain. We didn't have tents, just little lean-to shelters and we would camp on the river. You didn't have ice and ice boxes, but we had what we called "fish boxes." It was a box made with slats where you could sink it in the water and you would put the fish you caught in it. They would stay alive until you were ready to eat them. That was some of the best times of my life.

The place we fished on the Tombigbee was once Indian Territory. The Creek Indians first settled all that section of Alabama, where old St. Stephens is. There were old lime rock cliffs on the riverbank, high cliffs 60 to 70 feet high. Out from under those cliffs, there would be caves and I used to go and look in them. There would be springs-limewater-coming out of those old caves and that's what we used to cook with. There were holes hewn out in that soft lime rock and that was what the Indians used for bathtubs. It was like a water container. The spring would run down through it and you could dip water up out of there and that's what we cooked with. I won't ever forget that was some of the best times of my life. That fish, blue catfish out of the Tombigbee River, would make a tadpole spit water in a whale's face.

We don't like to reflect back on sorrowful times, but there were times of sorrow, too, during this period. My granddaddy Bailey had a sister named Mag. She never married, she had polio and her right arm and leg were crippled, but she went on and did the best she could. She was a wonderful person and loved me very much. Some of the fondest memories are of getting off the school bus and finding she and my Grandmother Bailey had cooked some good cornbread to go with our milk. They had a milk cow and would skim the cream off the milk and have it with cornbread. Doing that is such a good memory. In later years, my Aunt Mag was the first to become sick. She never recovered and died at the age of 82. She taught me so much.

Her daddy was Lige, my great granddaddy, who was the Confederate veteran. I had the old letters where he wrote back home from the army camps where he was in service from Mobile, from Tennessee and from Ohio. Aunt Mag, who was his sister, was the little girl that he would be writing. She had told me so much about the Baileys. She told me they originally came from Kentucky. Her granddaddy, Tom Walker Bailey, had a tanning factory on the Tombigbee River. She would tell me about riding the stage coach line. Now all this is a lot of history, but it is really real. I still live about one-fourth mile from the Old Gib Bailey Place. The stage coach line went right by there. In fact, my granddaddy Gib Bailey and Annie Melissa Mosley moved in the old stage relay station when they got married. It was an old hotel and relay station and they lived there awhile. My Aunt Mag lived with them and she would tell me about riding the stage coach line with the drivers up to her granddaddy's place on the river at the relay station and then riding the next stage back. I go there, even now. The signs of the old road are still there and sometimes I'll go there and just sit and think about the good times.

It was a very sorrowful time when I lost her. I was right by her bed when she died. That was the first person I ever saw die. You always remember that.

A few years later, my granddaddy Bailey, who was her baby brother, came down with what we thought was sugar diabetes and maybe cancer, too. Back then, a diagnosis was hard to come by and he was just a very sick man. We sat up with him at the old home place as long as he could go. Then when he got so sick we moved him to our place by oxen cart. I won't ever forget that little two-wheel cart. We went to pick him up and he wanted to look at the place one more time. He said, "I don't feel I'll ever get to come back." He and my grandmother got on the little old cart. I remember the names of the oxen were "Spot" and "Bully." We carried them to my mother and daddy's house. They stayed with us until he died. He didn't live much longer after that. He never did get to go back home.

My mother's only brother was E. H. Bailey. He

gave me my first Christmas present. We called it a "stopper gun." It shot pieces of cork that we called "stoppers," because at the time they were used to seal bottles, usually bottles of medicine. It was a little double-barreled shotgun. It didn't shoot; it just had stoppers in there. Aunt Mag would help me. She'd go squirrel hunting with me with that gun. Oh, I thought, I was going on one of the biggest hunts you ever saw when we'd walk down through the woods and she'd let me make believe I was shooting squirrels. Such are childhood memories that you won't ever forget.

Chapter 2

Washington County, Alabama and Private Gibeon J. Sullivan

Washington County, Alabama's rich and colorful history began June 4, 1800, when it was created by a proclamation of Governor Winthrop Sargent of the Mississippi Territory, making it the first county government to be established in what would later become the state of Alabama. The original boundaries of the county measured 300 miles east to west and 88 miles from north to south and it contained 25,000 square miles. From this area 16 counties in Mississippi and 29 counties in Alabama have been formed in whole or in part.

On March 3, 1817, the United State Congress established the Alabama Territory and Washington County gave birth to the first and only territorial capital, St. Stephens.

The county was named in honor of General George Washington. Today the County is located in the southwestern part of Alabama and is bounded by Choctaw County to the north, the Tombigbee River to the east (across which lies Clarke and Baldwin Counties), by Mobile County to the south, and by the State of Mississippi to the west.

For centuries the Gulf of Mexico Coast was the scene of international rivalries. The area which became Washington County was claimed by Spain as part of Florida from 1519 to 1700; governed by France as part of Louisiana from 1700 to 1763; taken from France by England in 1763 and held until the end of the American Revolution when it was regained by Spain.

The Treaty of Paris ended the American Revolution in 1783 and left the new United States without any coastline on the Gulf. Spain lay claims to some, the United States to other and the State of George claim title to yet more.

Claims began to clarify in 1795 when Spain withdrew and in 1798, the U.S. created the Mississippi Territory, which included this area.

Only two population centers existed in the Mississippi Territory, Natchez on the Mississippi River and the Tombigbee settlements at the forks of the Tombigbee and Alabama Rivers. The territory was divided into the Natchez District, west of the Pearl River, and the Tombigbee or Mobile District, east of the Pearl River.

St. Stephens, about 50 miles north of Mobile, served as the capital of the Alabama territory. When Alabama was made a state, St. Stephens served as the first county seat for Washington County. The county seat was later moved to Chatom, where it is now located, because it was more centrally located for the residents.

Gibeon J. Sullivan was born December 29, 1831 at St. Stephens, AL. He was the first Sullivan to inhabit Washington County.

He owned a small farm on Bassett's Creek, but his main support for his large family was working for wages on any public work available.

During the War Between the States (1860-65), Wilson's Guards, a Confederate Infantry Company, was recruited in St. Stephens in December 1861 and in January and February 1862. All enlistments were for the duration of the war. When the 32nd Alabama

Infantry was organized in Mobile in April 1862, Wilson's Guards, 87 strong, became Company A of the regiment.

Sullivan and his brother-in-law, Alexandria Lane Jr., were working on railroad construction in Baldwin County at the time the guard was formed, according to *The History of Washington County*, by Jacqueline Anderson Matte which was published by the Washington County Historical Society in 1982. Both men left their work and enlisted.

According to the book, "Private Sullivan was a man of great strength and during the conflicts he seems immune to enemy fire, disease or hardships. Even in military prison, during the last year of the war, it was said of him that he could "eat and fare" and thrive on it, something few could do. He became color bearer of his company and when his regiment waded the Tennessee River at Bridgeport he carried Captain Robert Leroy Bowling across the water on his shoulders. Also, on the march when orders were received to advance at the double quick, he would hasten to the front of the company, hoist Captain Bowling upon his shoulders and carry him forward seemingly with little effort. In January and February of 1863, he was on detached duty as a sapper and miner. In January 1864 he was reported on extra duty with Pioneer Company, but his luck ran out in the Battle of Nashville."

During the second day of the battle, December 16, 1864, during the late afternoon, a portion of the Confederates became engulfed and surrounded by advancing Federals and a large number of men were taken prisoner.

Among the prisoners from Company A were Privates Sullivan and Elijah H. Bailey. They were immediately sent to Camp Chase Military Prison at

Columbus, Ohio. Private Theodore C. Bowling on March 12, 1865 joined them there. He was the oldest son of their former Captain.

According to Ms. Matte, "No attempt was made to record the hardships of the Confederate soldiers in this military prison. Suffice to say there are 2,199 graves of Confederate soldiers in the cemetery at Camp Chase. The men of Company A reported only one act of kindness while there. In the late spring of 1865, the prisoners, hungry for something green, were reaching for grass at the extreme outer edge of the compound. A guard on duty pushed some grass with his foot so that it could be reached by a prisoner."

Prisoners were released in June 1865 after taking the Oath of Allegiance to the Federal Government. The release papers on Private Sullivan provide a physical description: Complexion, dark; hair, dark; eyes, blue; height, 6 ft 2 3/4 inches; and age, 35. There was an "X" mark by where his name was signed.

Upon their release, the three soldiers from St. Stephens made their way home the best way they could, mostly on foot.

Ms. Matte wrote, "They reported that they had a very bad time until they reached Kentucky. After that the people were kind to them. One time they were allowed passage on a river packet for part of the journey, but being ashamed of their unkempt appearance isolated themselves from the other passengers. They were given food, which they spread upon the deck, seating themselves around it. On learning their identities, the packet captain strode forward, kicked the food overboard, took the ragged soldiers to his own table and treated them as honored guests."

Private Sullivan had carried Captain Bowling on his shoulders across the streams he forded on the way into Tennessee three years earlier. Now, he carried his captain's ill son across the streams on the long journey home.

Private Sullivan died November 1, 1914. Following his death, St. Stephens Lodge No. 81 erected a modest tombstone over his grave in Clearwater Cemetery on Bassett's Creek. His epitaph is as follows:

To our Brother, G. J. Sullivan.
A Confederate Soldier, a Mason, and a man
In every sense of the word.

Chapter 3

Margie Louise Brewster

I am not ashamed to say that I am a sharecropper's daughter. I am the sixth of 12 children born to Otis Leon and Ruby Alma Givens Brewster. They were married July 2, 1922 and I was born January 22, 1933.

My grandfather, Alec Givens, (my mother's father) died from scarlet fever at the age of 37 in Brookhaven, MS. This left my grandmother (Cornelia Wilson Givens) with a family of six children to raise.

In those days there was no Social Security and they were hard pressed just to survive. My grandmother's brother, Shelby Wilson, went to Lecompte, LA where there was a lot of work in the logging industry. My grandmother followed and took a job at a hotel as a cook for the men who stayed there. My father and his family were also there working and that is how my mother and dad met.

When logging played out in Lecompte, my dad began to farm. In those days there was no modern means of farming like there is today. There was no commercial fertilizer and many people had trouble making their crops grow. To tell the truth, I think my daddy was a very poor farmer but I am proud that I had hard-working parents, who did everything they could to be successful in life and to provide for their children.

My mother sewed for people and she also made beautiful quilts. No seamstress today can make quilts of the same quality as the ones she made, as far as I'm concerned. Mother used cotton to line the quilts, but the cotton was not in a roll like you buy it today. Daddy would gin cotton and bring it home. (When you gin cotton, the seeds are taken out.) He would bring sacks of the ginned cotton and they would make mattress pads out of it.

When making a quilt, my mother would take the cotton and pat it and make it extremely smooth and thin. There would be literally hundreds of pats on the lining before she put the top on it. Then she did the quilting by hand. There was rarely a time that Mama didn't have a quilt on the frames at our house.

She really had no spare time, but in the minutes that she could catch, she did a quilt or sewed. She had an old treadle machine that she sewed on. She put a lot of care and a lot of love into every stitch she sewed, because not only did she want to please the people who bought her sewing, she took pride in doing good quality work. That was one thing she taught me; whatever you do, be sure it is done right and that's what I have always tried to do. In housework, washing, ironing, whatever task I do; I always try to do the very best job possible.

In fact, my parents taught me many things that I've appreciated all during my lifetime. You know, we never sat down to eat a meal that Dad didn't say grace, and we never went to bed before first gathering in the living room where the fireplace was and having family prayer.

Daddy always raised a garden. We had good produce to eat, such as peas, butter beans, tomatoes and okra. During the summer we "laid by the crop." Now, for some of you youngsters, I will explain what it means to "lay by the crops." All during the spring and early summer, we worked the crops and "laying by" means that we worked them one final time before the vegetables were harvested. By July 4th we always tried to have the crops "laid by."

When the garden came in, we always had plenty of canning to do. My mother made all types of preserves. We picked blackberries and she made blackberry jam and jellies. We gathered mayhaws, a wild fruit that grows in low areas around water. Our's grew around a little pond. They fell from the trees and looked like tiny apples. They made the best juice in the world. We would get wild plums and Mother would make jelly from them. When we could get peaches, we canned them too. Her peaches were so good. The peaches and a pan of biscuits made a fine breakfast.

Mama would can tomatoes and make what we called "tomato gravy," and I still love it today. I serve it to my guests, because it reminds me of "the good old days." They really were good days. They were hard days, but they were wonderful days too. We were taught how to work and how to be honest and fair and how to treat our neighbors with respect. Back then, you had real neighbors and they all came when you had a problem. By the same token, we all went to help our neighbors when any of them had difficulties.

I'll never forget when I was nine and my baby sister, Doris, was seven. We were very close, but you know how sisters fuss and fight. We did that, but we still loved each other dearly. I always thought she was so pretty. She had fair skin, pretty blue eyes and blonde hair. She got sick around the first of June and died in July.

This was the first death I ever had to deal with. She had a hernia type problem that closed up her intestines. Infection set in and she developed gangrene and it killed her. I never will forget, my dad's sisters kept saying, "Honey, you need to touch her and tell her good-bye." That was so hard to do. I remember kissing her and I remember how cold she was. That was my first encounter with the death of someone I loved so dearly.

As I was growing up, we moved from place to place. Daddy was always trying to hunt a better deal and have more income for our family. He never worked a public job during his lifetime. He only went to the third grade in school and did not have the education necessary to hold a public job. However, when you know about the people of that era the way I do, you know they weren't ignorant by any means. They just did not have a formal education. They usually figured things out for themselves and they made things work out even when it looked as if it were impossible. My family moved several times. Just before I was born, they moved to Franklin Parish, in Northeast Louisiana.

We had little contact with doctors. Everyone used home remedies. We had to get by the best way we could because money was so scarce. A real doctor delivered only one of my brothers and sisters.

The only transportation we had was by wagon. Yes, a wagon with a team of mules carried us to church, the cotton gin and the store, unless we walked. There was only one car in the community. A man named Mr. H.A. Hemphill owned it. He was a very good man and if anyone got sick, we knocked on his door anytime, day or night, and he always took the sick person to the hospital. Other than that one car in the community, we lived in a very primitive way. I'll guarantee you one thing though, we stayed in shape. We didn't need to worry about a diet or losing weight. With all the farm work, walking back and forth to the store, post office and school; we just stayed in good shape.

In the early 1940's World War II started and my oldest brother, Chester, was drafted into the army. Before that time, the older siblings were married, but they lived close enough that we could see each other on a regular basis. When our grandmother, or my dad's sisters, or any other members of the family came, there was no way for them to let us know they were coming. When they came it was always on a Sunday because that was the day everyone visited.

They had to leave home very early in their wagon pulled by mules, because they lived several miles from us. Their family spent the day and then they had to leave early enough to get home before dark. The time we visited was always "premium time."

There was always a lot of visiting to catch up on and my mother fixed a big dinner. That's how she learned to make those good coconut pies and cakes that nobody else in the world can make the way that she did. Then, of course, she took those good peaches she canned and made peach cobblers that would just melt in your mouth. We had chickens and we would run one down and kill it to make dumplings.

We had a meat barrel and in the wintertime we killed hogs and used the barrel to salt down the meat. In the bottom of the barrel was a hole. In the barrel we would alternate stacking the meat and the salt. We would also put pepper in it, of course. Up in the mountains, they still use this same process to cure their meat. We had salt meat, which was really pickled, and there was no way that it could ruin. We went to the barrel to get bacon for breakfast. We called it middling back then. We boiled it to get all the salt out and then fried it. Daddy had a smokehouse where he smoked mostly hams and shoulders.

When there was a "hog killin" day, the neighbors came over and helped. The women got together in the kitchen and started making biscuits. As the men killed the hogs, they brought the livers and the ribs in. The women cooked and served biscuits, syrup, peas and whatever else they could put together. It was a real feast.

We canned meat. My mother fried sausage and took the grease and poured over the sausage to seal it. The sausage stayed fresh until time to eat them. She boiled meat by putting it in a pressure cooker. She boiled it in jars until it was tender and then sealed the jars. She then set the jars aside and later used the meat for gravies, dressing etc.

I'm telling you, we learned survival and we learned it at an early age. We all had chores. It took "all hands and the cook," as the old saying goes, to keep it all going. Naturally we had a hand pump. We pumped the water we needed for cooking, washing clothes, bathing and for the animals. I'll guarantee you, my friend, that I pumped many a gallon of water in my time.

We had to milk the cows twice a day; in the morning and evening. Milk was very important; it was a big part of our staple groceries back then. Of course, we used the wood cook stove. We always brought in stove wood to use. We brought it in every evening so it would be there for Mama to cook breakfast the next morning.

In the wintertime we had to have wood for the old fireplace in order to keep warm. It took an awful lot of wood. We always put wood on the end of the porch that was easiest to get to. Just as sure as you didn't bring in your wood for the next morning to get the fire going, you would be the one called on to build the fire. We learned early that when Daddy said, "get the kindling" and "get the wood in," he knew who was supposed to have done it. If you didn't do it, the next morning, you had to get out early, no matter if there was frost or snow on the ground, and get the kindling and wood and build the fire to start the day.

Then, of course, there was cotton chopping, hoeing, and in the fall, cotton picking. We also raised corn. We always raised field corn, because it covered both areas. By that I mean we canned it for us to eat and when it was dried, we gathered it for the animals.

Daddy always raised a patch of sugar cane. From that we made our winter supply of syrup. It was so much fun to go with Daddy. Our whole family enjoyed making the syrup. I remember how they cooked it and skimmed the top off until the syrup was so pretty you could look down and it would be almost clear - you could see yourself in the syrup while it was being cooked. We always had sticky fingers from tasting it.

In the wintertime we popped corn and made popcorn balls. We invited the neighborhood children over and made a big mess in Mama's kitchen. We made what was called "syrup candy." We pulled it, and of course, we had a lot of fun and had more of it on us than we ate.

We bought coffee beans and Mother parched them in the oven and ground them. This was the best aroma ever. We loved the smell of coffee beans roasting even before we learned to drink coffee. My mother had a certain pan she parched the beans in and she had a stove rake that she used to rake it around in order to get all the coffee beans equally brown. Then it made delicious coffee.

We had a few "treats" to go with our daily fare. One of these treats was named Hershey's Chocolate on the can, but we just called it "cocoa" back then. The first chocolate we had was a real treat and also the first Kool-Aid. We didn't have any ice. We had an old icebox and when the iceman came around my mother would buy a 50 or 100 pound block of ice. When it ran out, we were out until the iceman came back.

I remember the first year I went to school. We always walked. Back in those days, in the remote areas where most of the sharecroppers lived, there was no school bus to come pick us up. The first school I attended was at Gilbert, LA. We had to cross a ferry and walk and it was a mile and one-half each way. All the kids in the neighborhood walked together and other kids joined us as we walked by their houses. If snow was on the ground we would fight and throw snowballs - just for fun. We laughed and talked and had a good time walking to and from school. In the winter months we had to hurry to get home in time to do the chores before dark. Most of the time, we either ran or got in a "high lope" going home in the afternoon. At night, we got our lessons by the light of a coal oil lamp because there was no electricity in our home. I remember the first time we got electricity in about 1945. I was amazed by the way it worked.

I went to school until I was in the ninth grade. That was about the time my father died. I took correspondence courses to finish high school. However, I really got my education, such as I have, on the road. That's where I learned a lot.

For entertainment, the children played hopscotch, which we learned at an early age. We had jump rope also. Daddy let us use one of his plow lines for a jump rope. We enjoyed that very much. We were active. We jumped fences and we had a horse we rode. Daddy would take the mules to the field to bring the cotton back to where the wagon was, so he didn't have to carry those heavy sacks. He would let me ride the mules. My Dad and I had a really close relationship.

We seldom had a bought toy; we made our own fun. I got a doll for Christmas when I was about ten and that was the first doll I ever owned. I don't know what ever became of her. I left her at home when I set out on my own.

I had a tea set once and that was a lot of fun. I played with the other children and I served them. It was all make believe, because we had no tea. We read in books how the English people served tea. My mother made teacakes and that was a real treat at our house. We played as if we had tea in our cups, but it was only water.

I'll never forget our mules. Their names were "Jack" and "Ada." When you had mules, you loved them, or at least I did. But of course, I love all animals. Mules carried heavy loads for people, like a pickup truck does today. The mules did a lot of heavy work for their master.

Daddy told me one day, "Now baby, I'm puttin' the cotton sacks on the mule and I want you to ride the other mule and take it to the wagon where we can weigh it." We always had to weigh the cotton so we would know how much to put in the wagon to make a bale. If I remember correctly, it would take about 1,200 to 1,400 pounds of cotton in the wagon to make a bale. That would gin out to make a 500 pound standard bale.

Daddy loaded the mule with all the sacks and I got on the other mule to go to the wagon. Well, somewhere going down the middle of the cotton field, which we had already picked, one of the sacks on the bottom caught a cotton stalk and pulled every one of those sacks off and out into the field. The sacks had been tied to keep them from emptying. There I was with those mules and all of the cotton on the ground. I knew Daddy was depending on me and I knew some of those sacks must weighed 100 pounds or more, but I took them one by one and put them on the mule. I got them back like Daddy had fixed them and got them to the wagon. There was one thing I never wanted to do and that was to disappoint my daddy. He really believed in me. I was the one, and I don't mean that he was partial, but he knew he could depend on me. If he sent me to the store with the last dollar he had, I always came back with his change. We just had a great relationship.

I will never forget when we lived in an area where we could hear radio station KWKH in Shreveport, LA. Those were the years of the famous Louisiana Hayride country music show where so many of the entertainers were on KWKH live each day. I was privileged to hear Johnny and Jack, Miss Kitty Wells, and the Bailes Brothers. They all made a great impression on me. I loved their harmony and I loved the heart-felt songs they sang. At one time, Mac Wiseman was there, as were Charlie Monroe, Hank Williams and many of the great ones of that era. Many of the great stars in country music started on the Hayride. Webb Pierce started at the Hayride. I heard him before he ever went to the Grand Ole Opry.

On this particular occasion, the Bailes Brothers came to the school at Baskin, LA to perform. I don't think I ever wanted to see anything as badly in my life. All I had to do was climb on Daddy's knee, put my arm around him and ask if he had any money. If he did, I could get the last penny he had, but at this particular time he didn't have enough money for me to go.

I didn't get to see the Bailes Brothers that night, but in later years I met them and to this day, we still have a great relationship with the two that are left, Walter and Homer. There were four boys and one girl. Homer played fiddle; the late Johnny Bailes was the lead singer, master of ceremonies and played guitar. Walter played guitar. Ernest Ferguson played mandolin and Shot Jackson played the steel guitar. Their only sister, Minnie sang with them for a long time. She had a voice that reminded me of the late

Mother Maybelle Carter.

We rarely had money for special events such as the Bailes Brothers performance, but we always had love in our home. We had consideration for one another and we were taught good manners. We were taught to say "Yes, Ma'am" and "No, Ma'am" and "Yes, sir" and "No, sir." This is a habit I still have today, especially with older people. We were taught to honor and respect our elders, our preacher, our school teachers and our elected officials. Back in those days you could respect them as almost all of them had high morals and standards and they expected you to live up to those same standards.

The first memories I have of music are from church. We didn't have radio or television so the only contact we had with music was when we went to church. There were people who sang beautiful music and someone would bang around on an old guitar. The only accompaniment the choir had was that old guitar and sometime we might be blessed enough to have a piano player join in.

I suppose the first music I heard was my daddy playing guitar. The first singing was my mamma singing to me. There was always singing around our house. We didn't own a guitar, but we had a neighbor by the name of Alonzo Mayberry, who had a guitar. Real early in life, Dad would send one of us to borrow the guitar and, of course, Alonzo and his wife, Edna would come with the package. We all gathered at our house and sang gospel songs until way in the night.

I'll never forget the first guitar I owned. I was 13 years old and it was just before my dad's death. We had a big cotton crop in the field. That was in the days we raised mostly cotton and it was our money crop. Dad knew I was a good cotton picker and he knew how badly I wanted a guitar. He promised if I helped him, which I always did anyway, that when he ginned the first bale of cotton and sold the seed, I could have my choice of a watch or a guitar. Naturally I chose the guitar. It was the first one I used when I started in gospel work. My mother bought it from Montgomery-Ward and I can remember the cost was $15. It had a real thin cardboard case. Fifteen dollars back then is like $150 or more now. I now realize that it was part of the money that was needed to carry the family through the winter. Dad, being a musician and singing and playing like he did, was so proud that I loved music and wanted me to sing and play like he did. I realize that my love of music made him so proud that he sacrificed to get the guitar for me.

Today they name guitar-playing styles after people and I would say that my daddy used the Merle Travis style. He used three fingers, but he didn't use picks. In years past, before my Dad was converted, people from near and far came and got him to play for community dances.

They had their own kind of entertainment back in those days. There were no big shows to go to and if there had been, people wouldn't have had the money to go, even if there was a show just around the corner. They made their own fun and entertainment. It was always good, clean fun. They loved to dance, I think it was just something everyone loved to do. The men did a lot of buck dancing and they also did waltzes and partners danced together. Then of course there were the square dances and you needed a fiddler for them. I'll tell you what, when I first heard the Grand Ole Opry, the music made by Sam and Kirk McGee and people like that, it was exactly like the music I'd heard during the years I was growing up.

In the summertime, we almost roasted while cooking on the wood stove. We learned to get up early and cook our breakfast and at the same time cook our dinner. We had a warming closet on the stove where we put our food to stay warm until lunchtime. The stove usually set, not right in the corner, but cat-a-corner. We filled our bathtub from the stove's reservoir and it was good and warm. Everyone bathed in the same water, the little ones first and then the bigger ones.

We put milk in the spring where we got water or we pumped water as cold as we could pump it and set the milk down in it because it would sour in just a short time if we didn't keep it cool.

We learned to take care of our clothes. When we came in from school, the first thing we did was pull off our dress clothes. I can remember I always wanted to have enough dresses so that I didn't have to wear the same one to school twice during the week. My mother remedied that by making me some skirts. I would change skirts and usually wear the same blouse, a lot of the time. Can you imagine the clothing that it took for 12 children, plus Mama and Daddy? Think about how many pair of shoes. Can you imagine washing all those clothes?

Monday was wash day. We had to pump the water for the washing. We had an old wash pot that we boiled the clothes in. I'll guarantee you, they were just as sanitary as the ones you wash in your washer today. Back in those days, we didn't have bleach. We had Octagon Soap, which we bought at the store. It was yellow and was made from lye. And, of course, we made our own soap. That stuff was so hard on our hands and we didn't have lotion, so we had chapped hands all the time.

We washed on a wash board and we boiled our clothes in a pot. Someone built a fire and filled the pot with water and clothes and we started the washing. It took all of us, because my mama could not do all of that "rubbin'" for all of the family, so each of the kids took a turn at the washboard. We washed them on that old washboard with the soap. I have seen my knuckles bleed from rubbing. We had what we called "bluing." It was an agent, in a stick like a crayon. We put it in the rinse water and it acted like bleach. It made the clothes pretty and white. It took a whole day to wash and if it was high humidity as it is prone to be in Louisiana it would take two or three days for the clothes to dry.

In our family, the first child born was my brother, Chester, then another brother J. L., and then a sister Nell. The fourth child, a brother, was named Earl. I never knew him because he died. Then there was another brother, Clyde. I was the sixth child. By the time my Dad died, my oldest brother had married and moved five or six miles from us. That was Chester, the one who went to service. J. L. was born next and he passed away at age 50 in 1975. He too had already married by the time Dad passed away. Then my oldest sister, Nell came along. She is married and lives in Thorndale, Texas. Next came Clyde, who was just two years older than me. He went into the service and served in the Korean War. He was shell-shocked and had constant flashbacks from the war until his death. He died at a very early age, about 50, in 1978. He and I were very close while we were growing up.

There were seven of us still at home when Daddy died. I remember Mama prayed a lot. She continued to make quilts and clothes for people, just so she could support the family. She was a very good manager. She continued to have a garden and a cow. The older children who were married helped her financially. My dad had no Social Security so my mother got $44 a month from welfare.

There was a lot of work, but it was seasonal. In the spring, in March, we planted corn, cotton, and the other crops we raised, as well as the garden. We harvested the garden when most of the work for the springtime was done. Then we started harvesting the other crops, which ripened in the fall. So we had some time in between spring and fall and that's when revivals came to our country.

I remember the first revival I ever attended. Until that time our church going was sporadic. It was just once in awhile when somebody came by and took us, or when they had a revival in the area that we could attend. Sometimes, if the weather was good, Daddy would take off early in the afternoon and we'd put our best clothes on, hitch the mules to the wagon and head for church. The Rev. J. A. Hawthorne preached the first revival I ever attended. He was from Winnsboro, LA and came to Baskin, LA and built what they called a "brush arbor." This was a tent-like structure made of poles and covered with small bushes having leaves to provide shade. I went to the revival every night as it was within walking distance.

Brother Hawthorne played the fiddle and this was the first time I ever heard the fiddle used with gospel music. He was a good song leader. He sang old songs like *Jesus Hold My Hand*. The congregation just came alive when he sang; you could just feel the songs in your heart. This was the prettiest singing I ever heard. *Will The Circle Be Unbroken, Just Over in the Glory Land* and numbers like that are still my favorite songs.

Then Brother Hawthorne would preach. He was one of those hell-fire and brimstone preachers. He preached that hell was hot; he preached that Heaven was a sure thing and he made you want to go there. That's when I was converted; in a brush arbor meeting. I'll never forget the night he preached. I even remember his text to this day: "If you die in your sins, where I am, you can not come."

47

I thought about how wonderful it is to love the Lord and although I was only nine that really hit home with me. I knew I did not want to go to hell and that I did not want to be eternally lost. So they sang *Kneel at the Cross* at the end of the preaching and I knelt at the altar.

Half a child, I thought how proud I'd be if they'd gather around and pray with me, but after awhile I started praying for myself. I really didn't need anyone to pray for me because this had to be between the Lord and me. This is the way it really is. It's a one to one thing. When you really get down to business with the Lord, He's right there. He's there to touch you, and He touched me and He blessed me and He cleansed me.

I know I was only nine and I had not done many wrong things in my life, but I had done enough that when I came into His presence, I felt guilty. I think the same thing is true today. When you come into the great and holy presence of the Lord, if there is guilt in your life, you really feel it. That condemns you. His spirit and His presence condemns you. So, when I knelt at that altar, it changed my life forever, because I was born again. I was filled with the spirit of the Lord. And I know that many people don't believe in it today, but a nine-year-old child spoke in tongues. I don't know what happened to my tongue. I spoke in another language. I couldn't understand what I was saying. I don't know if anyone around me understood or not, but I know I spoke in a heavenly language. That experience with the Lord changed my life forever.

During that revival, I went to the creek for an old-fashioned baptizing. Back in those days we didn't have a church of the Pentecostal faith, we only had that brush arbor. There were no baptisteries in churches in those days; people went to the creek. We had an old-fashioned baptizing and I was baptized in the name of the Lord Jesus Christ for the remission of my sins at nine years of age. That was, I don't know exactly how to say it, the most profound thing in my life; my personal experience with the Lord. It changed my direction.

I had already learned to play the guitar and that pleased my daddy so much. I started singing songs that I heard on the radio, mostly what they played on KWKH. We never had a victrola or a means to play records in our home. But when I got to my grandmother's (Nelia Givens) house, my mother's mother, that was a different story. She had an old victrola and she had lot of old 78 records, like the Bluebird label. She had records by Bill Monroe and Roy Acuff. I heard songs like the *Great Speckled Bird* and *This World is Not My Home*. The latter, I believe, was the first gospel song that Bill and Charlie Monroe ever recorded. They then recorded *Mansions for Me*, which was good. I learned all those songs and I wrote them by hand in books. I still have these books. I've kept them all these years. The ink is so faded that you can not read them. Those copies are very precious to me because they were the first songs I learned. Every song I heard, I wanted to write down. I never wanted to forget the tune. I had no knowledge of notes or how to read them. The only thing I could do was copy the words and remember the tune. I was looking at those old books not very long ago. I have them in a cedar chest at the house. At the bottom of a page, I had written, "This is in the tune of such and such." In that way, I didn't let them run together. I could keep the tunes separated.

I was a good student in school and made straight A's. The only time I made a bad grade was in the ninth grade in algebra class. During the first of the school year we had to stay out and work on the farm and gather the crops. Anybody that ever studied algebra knows you learn something new every day. I got 30 days behind. It did not distress me because I knew I could catch up once I got a chance.

However, other events changed that. My seventh grade teacher was very interested in me. In fact, after my dad passed away, she tried to adopt me. She went to see my mother. She wanted to see that I had a good education and offered to send me to Louisiana State Normal College in Natchitoches, LA. She was an unmarried lady named, Lillian Corley, and she took care of her elderly father. But my mother wanted to keep us all at home and all together and I am proud of her for that. I think she made the right choice because I had to make a choice a little later and I think I made the right one also. Miss Corley wanted me to become a teacher like her. If I had gone into any other profession, I would never have been involved in the gospel singing ministry, which I have loved and been active in for so many years.

I loved the school days and I loved the children. I have one picture when we were all in the sixth or seventh grade. Although it is just a small picture taken with an old 120 Kodak camera, I can still identify all the children I went to school with. I've wondered so many times what happened to many of them. After I left home and got into gospel work, I had very little contact with any of them. I loved them when I was growing up; we were like family. If we had a fuss, we got over it. Some of the boys would fight and then they'd shake hands and be friends again. That's the way it was in school during those days.

They ran two grades together and the same teacher taught both. By the time I finished the first grade, I knew the second grade and was promoted to the third grade. I didn't go into second grade. If you really wanted to learn in those days, you could learn both grades at the same time. I did the fifth and the sixth together.

There were about 25 to 30 students in the same room. In those days, a lot of the parents weren't concerned about education as they are now. Many of them did not push the children to go to school and it was not a law that they had to go. Many children missed out on an education.

School was one and two tenth mile from our door and we walked. It was in the little town of Baskin, LA., that consisted of a post office, two stores and the doctor's office. There was a grammar school and high school both on the school grounds. We had a good principal. I remember him so well. Now in those days, they would paddle you for being out of line. If you ever had to go to the principal's office, everyone was ashamed of you. You were supposed to come to school and behave. The rule my daddy had was, "If you go to school and get sent to the principal, or if the teacher has to send me a complaint about you, I don't care how much they whip you at school, when you get home, you are going to get another one from me."

When we went to our neighbor's house, we went by the same rule. We were never to ask for anything to eat, unless it was mealtime and we were invited to share the meal. We were to respect everyone—the teacher, principal, school building and the other children. We were to be on our best behavior at school, as well as at church.

When we went to church, all the family went in and sat on a bench. I tried to sit close to Mama and we all knew better than to make her take us outside. If she had to correct you for misbehavior, when you got home Dad corrected you also. Instead of a double blessing, you got a double whipping.

We continued with all the normal routines around the farm and then we were hit by another hard blow. My Dad became sick in the month of August. We did not realize how seriously ill he was. He was only 44 years old. In October he passed away. We had already experienced the death of my sister, Doris but never could I, in my wildest imagination, believe or entertain the thought that we would lose Daddy. He was the mainstay in our family. He was the one in our lives who really "rowed the boat." We loved him dearly. But the head of the house was gone, leaving behind my mother, who was wild with grief, and seven children, the oldest being only 15. I was 13.

It was bad enough that we no longer had Dad but to add to our grief, we no longer had the one who did the farming and handled the crops. We were only tenants (sharecroppers) so for the owner of the land we were living on, it meant any income he would have had from the farm could no longer be fulfilled. Therefore, the crop in the field at the time of Dad's death, basically cotton, we picked, had it ginned and from the sale of the cotton we got enough money to pay for Dad's funeral expenses. This left no money for us to live on throughout the winter and we had to move.

Through a contact my mother had with some church people in another community, we learned of a house we could rent. It was about 20 miles away. This meant we had to go to another school. When I had to leave my classmates and my teachers it was like tearing me away from family because I loved all of them dearly. The day we left was a very sad day for me.

It was hard on all the children, moving into a new community, making new friends and starting school in the middle of winter at the end of a semester. I can tell you, it was a lot for a 13-year-old to cope with—the loss of a father, knowing that our means of making a living was gone and loosing all contact with former teachers and classmates.

Loss of revenue caused my mother to be unable to buy the provisions we needed for school. I remember I dreaded so badly going to the new school with holes in my shoes and wearing a hand-me-down coat. I just couldn't accept it; I could not cope with the situation. I didn't want to drop out of school, but I didn't know what else to do.

My prayer life continued and I still felt an urge to do work for the Lord. That thought was constantly with me. I couldn't shake it off, but I didn't know how to begin. I had rarely been out of Franklin Parish, LA. I'd never ridden a bus nor had contact with outside people except at church when an outside preacher came for a revival. That was about all the contact I had except for listening to KWKH. I knew I had some musical talent, but never did I think I had enough to go into the entertainment field. That really was not my desire anyway. My desire was to use what little talent I may have as a ministry for the Lord.

The opportunity presented itself through an advertisement in a little Apostolic newspaper that we got our hands on. There was a lady evangelist who had finished Bible School and was ready to launch her evangelism ministry. She did not play or sing and needed a lady companion to travel with her and help with the revival work.

I answered the ad and in just a short time got a letter back. My mother insisted that she come to our house so she could meet her. I guess she wanted to screen her to see what kind of person she was. When the lady came, she stayed at our house for two days. Her name was Hazel Chain. She was very dedicated and very intent on doing work for the Lord. She was quite a bit older than I was and very dependable. My mother felt she could trust her to take care of me.

So we left Delhi, LA by bus - me with my little

guitar Daddy bought me, a Bible that had been given to me and the best clothes and shoes that I owned. I had to promise my mother that I would stay in constant touch by mail, because we didn't have a telephone. I did. From her letters I realized money was needed by my family. Any money I could spare from what I made, I sent home to help with the other children. My mother was only drawing $44 a month. My daddy never worked under Social Security, so the only thing my mother could rely on was welfare from the state.

By then my older brother, Clyde, had gone to Bastrop, LA and gotten a job in the paper mill. He was doing the same thing I was. My mother still had five children at home to provide food and clothing for and to send to school. We both felt it was our obligation to help Mother anyway we could.

My gospel work with Miss Hazel was one of the greatest influences in my life. She taught me so many things - how to conduct myself while we were on the road, proper behavior in many circumstances and the ropes in evangelistic work, so to speak, and she helped to shape my life for the future I would have in gospel music.

Chapter 4

Margie Meets Enoch

As I said previously, I left Louisiana with an evangelist minister, Hazel Chain, in 1946. We traveled around Louisiana and Mississippi and then we got the opportunity to go to a place we had never been before—Alabama. It was through these travels that I met an Alabama boy, Enoch Sullivan, who was to be my husband. He was 15 at the time and I was 13.

We were contacted by letter about coming to Alabama. The letter stated they did not have evangelism there and needed help very badly in their little church.

Miss Hazel and I headed for the little town of Sunflower, AL by bus. We began holding services in the home of Leo and Annabelle Gartman. Miss Hazel preached and I sang. They moved all the furniture out of their living room, put some seats in and we started a revival. By word-of-mouth advertisement, which was all we had in those days, the news about the revival spread. There were no radio stations nearby that we could use. People began to tell of the good preaching and singing and folks started to come "out of the woodwork."

Enoch's dad, Arthur Sullivan, came and brought Enoch and other members of their family. Miss Hazel found out they played and sang and asked them to take part in the music. I remember at that time Aubrey Sullivan, I believe, or maybe Jerry Sullivan, played guitar, and Brother Arthur Sullivan played mandolin and Enoch played fiddle. They did not go by the name "The Sullivan Family" as that was to come later. It was just Brother Arthur Sullivan and his boys.

I was very impressed with the group because I always loved band music. I especially loved fiddle music. Brother Arthur was so forceful in his singing and talking that you couldn't help but stand up and listen. He was one of a kind. He was a lot like Johnny Cash, his voice might not have been totally on pitch all the time, and he may have missed as many notes as he hit, but he could drive a point home. His preaching was also very, very forceful.

Enoch was extremely bashful and so was I. We would just kind of glance each other's way during the progress of the services. After church we would maybe say "hello" or "howdy" or something. That was about the extent of our courtship for two and one-half or three years. When we weren't in the Alabama area, I would write him letters, or he would write me letters. That's the way we courted, by mail.

We were back in Alabama for a revival in 1949. When we started the revival, the Sullivans came every night. Enoch came to see me and I'll be honest, I was glad to see him.

I guess from the moment I met him on, it was fate or the hand of the Lord that caused our meeting and caused us to be attracted to one another, not just because of the music altogether, but just an attraction there.

He asked me to marry him. I told him I would have to get my mother's permission because I was only 16 and had been traveling with Miss Hazel extensively since I was 13.

We talked and my mother agreed that if that was what I wanted, she would agree for us to get married. On December 16, 1949, Enoch and I tied the knot.

Chapter 5

The Beginning of
The Sullivan Family
The First 10 Years-1949-1959

ENOCH: It was Dec. 23, 1949 when the Sullivan Family made its first appearance on radio on WRJW in Picayune, MS. That was the beginning. Marge and I had been married about two weeks. On that first appearance was my father, the Rev. Arthur Sullivan on mandolin, Margie Sullivan on guitar, Enoch Sullivan on fiddle and Aubry Sullivan, Arthur's brother on guitar. It was a minister, the Rev. Alvin Cobelentz, who was originally from Ohio, who actually had the program. We were guests on his show.

On that first show we met B. J. Johnson, who ranks high in the field of disc jockeys. He was one of the charter members of the Disc Jockey Association, along with people like Jimmy Swan, Boots Barnes, Jack Cardwell, Happy Wainwright and people like that who were radio personalities in 1949. B. J. was working as an announcer on WRJW at the time and he remained our friend all the way through. We were able to record in his studio at times. He produced our first live album with guests Carl Story, Marty Stuart and Carl Jackson. Mr. Johnson is deceased now, but he was a very outstanding disc jockey, well known in Nashville ranks.

MARGIE: I did a lot of the prayer requests on the programs, read the mail and gave our personal appearances. Enoch's dad was doing the emceeing and preaching. Enoch had very little to say except to 'talk on the fiddle.' I'll just have to say that's the way he did his talking. His dad was a sick man and had been having problems with his heart for quite awhile. He carried on the emcee work from the opening of the station until his death, about seven years later.

ENOCH: We met another man that day, Charlie Ballis, who was a disc jockey from Linden, AL. In early 1950 he opened radio station WPBB in our hometown, Jackson, AL. We went on the first day that station broadcast. We had a program of our own. On that first appearance was, of course, my dad on the mandolin, myself on the fiddle, Marge played the guitar and Dad's brothers, Aubry and J. B. both played guitar and sang some. My aunt Susie Bryant sang on that first broadcast and J. B.'s wife, Earlene, helped on the broadcast by reading the mail. We had a great friend, Hob Williams who sang and Hilton Taylor played bass fiddle. Hilton Taylor owned a hamburger shop in town and sponsored part of the program. I'd like to give them all credit, because that was a great evangelistic party.

MARGIE: Hilton Taylor was our first bass player. He worked regular with us for quite awhile, but he had his own business and sometimes he couldn't be with us full time. We had different ones to come in and help. Later, Enoch's brother Emmett, learned to play the banjo and joined us.

There is some confusion and it's hard for the fans to keep it straight especially if you don't know the facts and not everybody knows. Jerry Sullivan is Enoch's uncle. He married early and left home when he was 14-years-old. They had not named the group at the time. Nobody called them 'The Sullivan Family' until we went on radio. That's when we had a name for our group.

ENOCH: And I named it.

MARGIE: We never denied that Jerry was a part of the family, but he was not a part of the early broadcasts. He left home and was gone at the time.

ENOCH: For years he was gone. He married a year before Marge and I did and then Aubry married and he was gone. They married and left and then Susie married and left. She moved to Indiana and stayed a long time and she was never active in the group anymore. J. B. and Earlene left the group. Marrying, and I'm all for it, took most of the people out of our group. Later on death took some. With some members leaving the group, Marge and I were the ones that kept on dealing with it and working. Dad was a minister and he'd keep forging ahead and at his death, it was all ours. I mean it just dropped in our lap. We were in church and Dad died. The next weekend we had the radio broadcast to do. It was either go on or stop. And so somebody said, "You just as well go on up there and you all go on ahead." There wasn't nobody else to go but Marge, Emmett, and me 'cause all the rest of them had left home. They weren't even in the country. They just came home for the funeral and when it was over, they went back to their homes. That week came with Dad's death and the sorrow, the hurt and the heartache and then all at once here's tomorrow and its broadcast day. What are you gonna do? The radio station wants to know. Everybody wants to know. Well, somebody had to step up and there wasn't anybody to step up but Marge, Emmett and me.

My dad was the pastor of a church near town and we used the radio broadcasts to work out of and advertise our church services and guest appearances within the coverage of the radio station. When we got the program, we signed a 13-week contract and they had to know how to bill the program and what to call the band. It was just a family band.

My mother was always a great fan of the Carter Family - Mother Maybelle, Sarah and A.P. Maybelle's daughters, June, Helen and Anita, were just young

59

girls back then and they were very popular in our part of the country and they were the only family group I could think of.

I said, "I know we won't ever be as popular as they are, which we are not, and there will never be anybody that famous, but it would be something easy to remember, just call us 'The Sullivan Family.'

So, that's what we did so they could give us the advance billings or 'promos' during the week for the Sunday broadcast. During the time we were on WPBB, which was seven years, we were also on WJDB in Thomasville, AL for five years. During that time the band members would change and sometime we would have special guests come in for the program. Dewey Coleman was one of those who came in and could sing and play the guitar. He worked a lot with the southern gospel people, but he sang a lot like Roy Acuff or Stoney Cooper. He was a good group singer, but also a good solo singer. He wrote a couple of songs that were really going good and he wanted to record them. Dewey started working with us on the radio program and doing personal appearances. He was with us a year or two.

MARGIE: We had different gospel groups that were on the program like the Atwood Brothers. Paul Atwood was a good mandolin player and Tommy Atwood learned his first notes on the fiddle from Enoch. He was a good singer and later became the tenor singer for the Florida Boys. They had an older brother, Bill, and they all became our good friends and came many times to visit with us on the radio programs. Others like the Reverend Claude Walters who had a good group called 'The Singing Christians' and so many others were our guests either on the programs or at church visits.

Enoch's father built two churches in Alabama,

which were near our home. During this period he continued to pastor both of them. One of them was the Victory Grove Pentecostal Church just out of Wagarville, AL. and Bolentown Pentecostal Church, where Brother Arthur died, about six miles out of Jackson, AL.

ENOCH: During that time we got a chance to get a contract with Revival Records out of California. In 1954 we recorded Dewey's songs for Revival. It was a 78-rpm record. Dewey sang and we did the music. We recorded it at a radio station in Frisco City, AL. My daddy was on mandolin and I guess that was the only studio recording he made. I played fiddle on the record, Dewey played guitar, Luke Griggers played bass and Emmett played drobo on one side and the five-string banjo on the other. That was our only session that Marge didn't play on. She was in the hospital having our second baby.

MARGIE: After the first recording we continued with radio work, personal appearances and going to churches and wherever the doors opened we always went. The Lord always seemed to bless our work and He always blessed us to do His work.

ENOCH: For the history of bluegrass gospel music, according to *The Bluegrass Unlimited*, a magazine that deals exclusively with bluegrass and bluegrass gospel music, Carl Story was a great factor in bluegrass gospel music. He first added the five-string banjo to his recordings in 1956 to make it bluegrass gospel, which was two years after we first recorded and did it with banjo.

MARGIE: We continued to do the radio broadcasts. We had two Sunday morning programs that promoted all the work we did. Back then, the stations were powerful and there weren't so many of them. They were clear and they reached a long way.

And people listened to them. People would call or write in their requests and get us to come and do their revivals.

We did a lot of 'old time' or 'old fashion' days, where they would have an all day program with preaching and singing and dinner on the ground. We'd do family reunions and things like that. Remote radio broadcasts were also popular back then. Businesses would have us come in and do a live broadcast from their location because it would cause people to come in to their business and hopefully buy something. We did a few concerts. Enoch was the one who really wanted to push the music. Of course, his daddy was pushing the ministry, the gospel.

ENOCH: I remember before Dad died in 1957 the radio broadcasts on both stations were going strong and we were pulling big crowds. Sometime they couldn't get them all in the building. I asked Dad to please let us try one time to charge an admission. He didn't want to do that, but we did. We had our first program that we charged an admission at the old Clara, MS high school auditorium. I guess it would seat five or six hundred and it was packed. I could see then that the people loved the music well enough they would actually pay to get in. Even thought it was successful, Dad couldn't fulfill what he wanted to do. He wanted to preach and you couldn't do that if you advertised a commercial singing. Now days it's more acceptable, so that part of it has changed. I wouldn't play a place I couldn't give my testimony.

That was a highlight. It was a good mark for bluegrass gospel music back then.

There was something else in the making back in those days. We were looking forward to a couple of good friends, Johnny Bozeman and Paul DuBose, starting their own publishing and recording company,

62

called 'Sandy,' in Mobile, AL. They contacted us to join their label. We went down and signed a contract to record in November 1957.

We thought the session would include Dad, Margie, Emmett and me. In rehearsing however, Dad told us to go ahead and work it up because we would be the ones doing that kind of work. We didn't know how true that was. He passed away in November.

We were right at the height of the very best of our life's work, then and now. We had revivals going, concerts and one night stands. But we lost Dad and it seemed like the end of the world.

MARGIE: On November 23, 1957 we lost Enoch's dad. I'll never forget the weekend of his death - it was Thanksgiving weekend. The weather was bad. We went up to the little Bolentown church on a Saturday night, I believe, and we had a wonderful service. I'll never forget we were doing an old song called *Sweeping Through The Gates*. Brother Arthur asked us to come up and sing it again. We sang it three or four times for him that night and then he started his sermon. I'll never forget his text: "Search the scriptures for in them you think that you have eternal life and these are they, which testify of me."

He never even closed the Bible. He turned around and spoke to Enoch, saying, "Son, pray. Get them to pray." We didn't know it, but he was having his fatal heart attack right then. He knelt at the bench behind the pulpit and there is where he passed away. They picked him up and put him in the car, but they pronounced him dead upon arrival at the hospital.

ENOCH: They suggested we wait until we got ourselves back together and set the recording session for January 1958. As low as we felt in spirit, I think it was the kick off to what's held us to this very day.

MARGIE: After Mr. Sullivan's death, there we were without a leader, so to speak. We depended on him to do the preaching, we had depended on him as our leader. When he was gone we found ourselves with nobody to ask what to do. You get all these feeling mixed up. We thought maybe we should stop the radio program. We thought maybe the work was all over, but it didn't work that way. People began to call and ministers began to say, "Children, you have to carry on, you can't stop. The work must not stop. The Lord called Brother Arthur home. He finished his work, but yours is ahead of you. You have yours yet to do."

Enoch became the emcee. We started on the radio. He became spokesman on the radio. And, if I might say so myself, he's turned out to be one of the finest emcees in the country. I really think he is one of the best. He has a way of making people understand what he's saying and he does it in a way that's unequaled by anyone else as far as I'm concerned. He's blessed. Many people have told me that there's no better emcee than Enoch and that he's equal to Lester Flatt and people along that line.

He started on the radio and I know he must have been scared that first Sunday after Brother Arthur passed away. We were all scared but we continued doing the radio work.

ENOCH: The first recording for 'Sandy' was a song titled *I Can See God's Moving Hand*. Margie recorded that as a solo on one side and on the other side we recorded *Happy On My Way*, a song I had written. In the studio Margie played guitar, Emmett on banjo, Paul Atwood on mandolin, Terrill Booker, a union musician from Mobile, AL on bass and me on fiddle.

MARGIE: I remember after Mr. Sullivan's death

64

we had the question of what to do about the recording. We pondered, "It's already set up, it's paid for and everything is ready, so what should we do?" We prayed about it, we talked about it and we decided the thing to do was go ahead and record.

ENOCH: They released that recording and *I Can See God's Moving Hand* went to the top 100 in the *Billboard* Country Music Charts, which was all you had in those days. That was before Faron Young started *The Music City News*.

MARGIE: That really encouraged us. We knew that we would record more songs and we knew that the Lord's blessings were upon our work.

ENOCH: We went from there up to Nashville, TN and we were on Ernest Tubb's Midnight Jamboree broadcast over WSM each Saturday night following the Grand Ole Opry. Justin Tubb, Ernest' son, hosted the program that night. We sang both songs and when we finished, Grant Turner, the announcer, came and talked to us. He wanted to know who we were, where we were from and how long we had been working. He asked me if the recording was just exactly as we featured it on the program keeping the music going by playing the breaks in between. Back then most gospel groups stopped and started between verse and chorus. He said he wanted some copies of the recording to use on his early morning show on WSM. Grant Turner remained, until his death, one of the greatest friends The Sullivan Family ever had. He always knew us and where we were from. It didn't make any difference if it was five or ten years since the last time he saw us. He's say, "Now don't tell me, I remember." And he always did.

That was the highpoint of the first 10 years of our career. We got our first record contract and had done the singing. The low point was the loss of my

Dad.   Paul DuBose and Johnny Bozeman are both deceased, but Johnny's wife Helen is still active in music. She is a wonderful lady and is president of the Country Music Association in Mobile, where we many times have played 'The Gulf Coast Opry.'

There were a couple of boys who played on our radio broadcast as guests that were as good as anybody on the Grand Ole Opry. They were Travis Prichard and Bob Weaver, both from Jackson, AL. They were young, I'd say about 18, but they were just great and solid as a dollar. They would guest with us and when we recorded they wanted to know where. So we gave them Johnny and Paul's number and arranged an appointment for them to see about recording. I told Johnny and Paul, "They're just as good as the Grand Ole Opry." One of the boys could do imitations. He could sing like Hank Snow, Ernest Tubb or anybody he wanted to.

They got a contract with Sandy and recorded *Tell 'Em No* and *Wake Up Little Susie*. It immediately went to number one in the charts. I remember that Paul DuBose and Johnny Bozeman both bought a brand new Cadillac. They went to the highest markets there were in country music with those boys and featured them on big shows in New York, Chicago, Hawaii, overseas, and everywhere.

Then Dot Records bought Sandy Records out. Dot had the Everly Brothers recording for them. When Dot bought them out, instead of Travis and Bob getting the song, the Everly Brothers got it.

I would like to say this, I want this always to be remembered. We had mountain music before we had bluegrass music. Bill Monroe was on the Grand Ole Opry with his Bluegrass Boys and they were on the Opry, not a bluegrass show. That was before bluegrass was named 'bluegrass' as a music and before the days of the bluegrass festivals. Mountain music such as that put out by Carl Story, Ralph and Carter Stanley and Jimmy Martin (he was not on the national scene at the time) and people like that were completely restricted to the mountain region. Their mountain music came from Knoxville, TN, Ashville, N. C. and the Appalachian Country up there. They were recording people like the Stanley Brothers, but the recording companies were not putting them out into the mainline distribution of country music and they're still not. We know about them, but they don't know about us.

MARGIE: We continued on with the radio programs. Radio was very popular in those days. Everybody had a radio before the days of television and everybody listened. We got mail from as far away as the programs would reach and we got invitations to come and perform. That's the way we got started broadening our music into a bigger area. We went for revivals, one-night programs, singings, preaching, family reunions, all day services, and fellowship meeting - wherever they needed gospel singing.

We always went on a free will offering basis. We never set a flat rate for our services for the Lord. It was always sufficient. Whatever He blessed us with, it was just enough. You might say that from the very beginning, it was a work of faith. It pleases the Lord for us to believe in Him and trust Him to provide our needs. He will fulfill His promises because the word said that what He promised, He would also perform. He said, "The worker is worthy his hire." So I've always believed that if we trust Him with our eternal soul, which is going to live on forever, why can't it be easy for us to trust Him with our material needs? I think it pleases Him for us to trust Him.

We continued and Enoch had a steady job until 1958. He was always there for the radio programs and the real important dates and for as many of the church dates as he could make. He always furnished us with a car with which to travel and an open account at the service station for gas and tires and whatever we needed when he couldn't go. We always had his full support to carry on when he couldn't be there.

But in 1958 he felt especially moved that we should go into the ministry full time and that is exactly what we did. He quit his job as a chemical engineer at Eagle Chemical Company in Mobile, AL. He held his job all those years, plus helped us with the radio work and as many personal appearances as he could and, of course, helped me at home. Neither of us had a job, except the job the Lord had instituted for us. We trusted the Lord to made the way and provide for us. For many years, there were just the three of us in the work - Enoch, Emmett and me. We all shared and shared alike and the Lord blessed us enough financially that we all made a living.

ENOCH: I can read *Bluegrass Unlimited* and I can read all the history of the music and it makes me really sick and weak to know that all the people that covered that kind of music were up there in that region where that music was. They'll give you the history of Ralph and Carter Stanley and tell you they've done this and they've done that and I'm not jealous and I'm not prejudiced, but it should be set straight. The only way we knew about them was because Jim O'Neil on the big 50,000 watt stations like KTHS in Little Rock, AR and XERF in Del Rio, TX and the stations on the Mexican boarder would put record offers on. Jim O'Neil had a record shop like Ernest Tubb. It was a headquarters for old time mountain music, country and gospel. Jimmie Skinner up in Cincinnati, Ohio, I believe had the biggest record shop in the world at one time.

The record companies had special offers and those of us who loved that kind of music could get them. Since The Sullivan Family was isolated down here on the Gulf Coast region, where rhythm and blues was prominent, we didn't have any coverage whatsoever. We were the ones who originated bluegrass gospel music and we were left without any outlet for it or mountain music or straight bluegrass. Back in those days we were the only group that did bluegrass gospel exclusively and nothing else. If there were others, there weren't many. Due to our faith and religious beliefs we did it strictly, we specified it was exclusive gospel. It was bluegrass, but we didn't call it bluegrass, it was just Sullivan Family style gospel.

MARGIE: We met a lot of people in those years who were connected with gospel music, but not many connected with bluegrass gospel singing. As far as I know, we were the only ones in that area who were playing the kind of music we played. Back then it wasn't named 'bluegrass,' it was just called country gospel or string band music. I guess the reason for this is because there was no separation between bluegrass and country at the time. Everyone thought Mr. Bill Monroe was a 'hillbilly' with a 'hillbilly band' and it was all kind of in there together until he made his statement. I think it was about 1962 that he said from then on that his music would be called 'bluegrass' and he named ours 'bluegrass gospel.' We didn't play with anything but acoustical instruments; there were no electrical instruments in our band.

ENOCH: Our kind of music didn't have any major record companies, maybe Dot and Starday. Starday was doing a lot for it through Goldie Hill and her brother Tommy. They understood there was string band music that needed recording, so they did a lot of Ralph and Carter Stanley, Carl Story, Don Reno and Bill Harrell and people like that. Then Jim O'Neil would package it and sell it on his offers on the 50,000-watt stations. Therefore when we heard his spots, we could order the music we loved and get it. Ralph

Stanley and the people up in the mountain region didn't know anything about us because down South there wasn't enough of us to get our music out. It was a lack of communications.

Bluegrass Unlimited and *Music City News* didn't exist back then. You only had *Billboard* and they just covered what the radio stations were playing and mostly what the Grand Ole Opry had. That was the biggest outlet for it.

To prove what I am saying, Bill Monroe came down in our area in 1963, but as late as the 1970's, we got Ralph Stanley to come down and work some dates with us in Louisiana, Mississippi and the edge of Texas. He told us it was the first time he'd ever been that far South. He'd been down to Live Oak, FL but he didn't know anything about this country back out in here whatsoever.

Chapter 6

The Troubadours

ENOCH: Being in the music business, we've been fortunate in that we were able to spend a lot of time with our family. In our gospel music work we were away a lot, but we always maintained home and we'd come home on a regular basis. We'd go out sometime and stay all week and sometime maybe two or three weeks and sometime even longer, but we'd be back home and our kids would be well taken care of while we were gone. My mother looked out for them while we were gone and when we came home it was always a happy time to see the little ones.   Each year during the holidays we had good times because we scheduled our work to where we could be home with the family. Looking back on it now, we've been greatly blessed.

My late brother Emmett put it like this, "Well, we played our music like we wanted to; the kind that we want to, bluegrass gospel; we booked the places we wanted to be; and in the final analysis, each year would be better and better." Just before his death, he said he was very pleased with our work and if he had a chance, he wouldn't change a bit of it.

The gospel work has afforded us to raise our families and send them all to school and they all graduated. Our oldest son went to college. We had just about average of what our neighbors had in the material things in life. We had a nice place to live, food, clothing, a way to travel, good instruments to play and good friends to play for. You just can't beat that.

MARGIE: That's exactly right, Enoch. I think Charlie Louvin put it so well when he said, "The most blessed people of all are the ones who can do a job they like to do and make a living at it."

A lot of people have to work in manufacturing plants and do jobs they don't really like, but it's necessary in order for them to make a living. We were blessed in that we loved music and we felt like we were called into the work and to be able to make a living for us and the members of the band were an added, great blessing that came from the good Lord.

ENOCH: When our family was young, the kids cried when we left, but Margie had a way of fixing it so they would be looking forward to when we were coming back instead of being sad about us leaving. She was always real good at special times. When the kids were real young they didn't understand about us leaving like they do now. They're all grown men and women now. They can look back now and they tell us how well they think we did with it. I give the credit to Marge, because she knew how to keep the family together better than I did.

It's amazing how it all worked out. In every family someone has got to make a living at something in different trades and occupations. Ours was gospel singing. Marge was good at booking the programs and staying in contact with the places we were going to play - mostly ministers, booking agents and promoters in the gospel business. She kept up that side of it and I kept up the farming part of it. I kept the automobiles ready to go as good as I could. I wasn't a very good mechanic, but I could keep us on the road. Outside work is what I enjoyed. Marge worked right along side me with the hard work too, but she enjoyed working inside with the family and keeping in contact with people. She always enjoyed cooking and still does.

MARGIE: The girls always had funny things to say about the way we managed. A lot of times in those years we had people come in unexpectedly to see us. What I had on hand was not very much to cook for a big group, because the children ate one way and when we had company we ate another way. The children liked hamburgers, hot dogs and French fries, you know how growing children are. We liked peas and corn bread, potato salad and chicken and so forth. I always made gumbo. We loved 'southern cooking.' Our middle daughter is now grown and has a family of her own. She goes to church, of course, and said one time the preacher's sermon was the Lord taking the five loaves of bread and the fishes and feeding the five thousand. She said she'd seen a miracle at our house, too. She said she had seen her mama take one chicken and feed 32 people. The Lord multiplied things around our house, too.

ENOCH: I heard a story along that same line. A good friend of ours, Homer Hodge was a deputy sheriff in Louisiana. His daughter had finished high school and he wanted her to go to college. She was a beautiful lady. A holiness preacher came to town and was holding a revival. Well, she met him, fell in love and wanted to get married, and she did - they eloped. Mr. Homer was so upset and wanted to do the preacher in. Some of us were trying to console him and someone said, "Homer, you don't know, it might turn out to be better than you think. After all, he's a preacher. She could have done worse than a holiness preacher."

He said, "I don't think so. My mother raised all 10 or 12 of us and there was a holiness preacher at our house at all times, it seemed like. I never will forget that she would fix the best we had. She would fry chicken and take the very best we had, make us all wait and feed those holiness preachers. They'd eat everything in sight. Why, I was 21-years-old before I knew a chicken had anything but a neck and a wing."

He was displeased at first, but everything turned

out all right. The man turned out to be a good preacher. I was able to ask him later on, "Mr. Hodge, what do you think about your son-in-law now?" He replied, "I'd have to think pretty well of him." He held up a set of keys in his hand and said, "You see these? I want to take you out and show you. I have a brand new three bedroom house, finished, with the keys handed to me and donated to me by my son-in-law and daughter." So I told him, "See, he turned out to be a better fellow than you thought he would." Things have a way of working out like that.

MARGIE: Our children have all married good people. We've made them a part of our family and that's just the way they act. If they come to our house and we've got something cooked and they want some, they know to get it. If they need a tool from Enoch, they borrow it. Whatever they need. If they need a vehicle, they borrow it.

ENOCH: And most of the time, never bring it back. When you raise five children and they all marry and you wind up with 13 grandchildren, you've got an awful lot of in-laws but they're all fine people.

MARGIE: We're real proud of all our in-laws and we're especially happy with the grandchildren. One of the greatest treasures at this stage in our lives is our little great-granddaughter, Katlyn Mariah Walker, who is three at this writing. Three going on 21. She has everybody in the family wrapped around her little finger.

Chapter 7

Whipping That Ole Cancer

ENOCH: I was diagnosed with cancer on July 3, 1960 and it was a real sad time because we had been working full time in the gospel field since 1958. It seemed that unless the Lord took control, I might not be able to continue in the work, or even in my life. I was really sick, but the Lord saw fit to send the healing that I needed; not instantly, but on a daily basis. I started mending and started getting better right away from the surgery and the treatments for the cancer. I just put my faith and trust in Jesus Christ and we kept working and going. Sometimes I wondered how long it was going to last. But I progressed and each year I wondered if I was gonna make it. Looking back now, we never know what tomorrow or next week or next year is going to hold. Looking back at that period now, I can see that in our work and in my health, each year was better than the one before. And in the music work each year we'd gain in contacts.

MARGIE: It was strange the way we became aware of Enoch's cancer. First of all, we bought a set of 1958 World Books for the children to study with. In the books, he had read about cancer and how you need to look for little lumps. We had been on the road and were off a few days. We always made our time at home premium time with the children. We'd get out and play with them and have a lot of fun together. The boys were batting the softball, one of them hit the ball and the ball hit the ground, bounced up and hit Enoch in the side. At the moment the ball hit him, he just touched his side and there was a lump, a knot. He never got easy from the time the ball hit him, to the point of being really sick to his stomach.

He was really concerned about it and so was I.

We didn't know what to do. A lot of people back in those days taught that you trust in the Lord with your illnesses. I know he was reluctant to go to the doctor, because at that time you tried not to offend anyone by any of your actions. But he prayed about it and prayed and prayed and he never got easy. He asked me, "What do you think I ought to do?"

I replied, "Now Enoch, you're asking me something I can't answer. I can't tell you what to do. You will have to come to that conclusion between you and the Lord. Whatever you do, if you go to the doctor, I will be there with you. If you decide to trust in the Lord, I'll be there with you in that. We'll fast and pray together. Whatever you want to do, we will do for you to get better."

The night before he went to the hospital he was like a worm in hot ashes. He could not get easy; not any way at all. Lying, sitting, standing, whatever, he couldn't get easy. So he told me, "If I live until morning, I'm going to see the doctor."

The doctor was a friend Enoch had gone to school with, so he didn't feel bad to go see him, Dr. Robert Bolan. The next morning he got up and after he was ready, Emmett and I carried him to the doctor. We had a singing date that night at Foxworth, MS at Brother Marvin Terrell's church. We decided we would all get ready, go to the doctor and then go on the program that night.

Dr. Bolan checked the knot and told Enoch, "I think I know what it is, but I'd rather not say. I want to send you to a specialist. I want you to go right on. I'm going to call now and make you an appointment to see him this afternoon."

We drove the 60 miles to Mobile, AL to get to Dr. Shep Jerome's office. He checked Enoch and said, "I'm almost positive I know what it is, but I would rather be sure. I want you to go to the hospital. We're going to do experimental surgery and remove the knot and see what it is."

We went on to the singing that night and it was easy to tell the wind had been about "knocked out of our sails." I think we all knew in our hearts that it was bad news. We asked the people to pray and we went on to the rest of the programs we had for the weekend.

On Monday morning we were at the hospital. They conditioned Enoch for surgery and operated on him the next day. I stayed with him and his mother and sister, Jewel, who was also real good help with the children, came. He had lots of company that encouraged and prayed for him. On Thursday he said, "I think you better go home and check on the children. I'll be all right. I think the worst of it is over."

I said I would, but for some reason I just couldn't leave. I didn't know why I was staying around. In a little bit, Jerry, Enoch's uncle, came in to see him and just as he stepped in the door, the nurse motioned for me to come outside the room. I don't think Enoch ever knew this because he was so proud to see Jerry. While they were visiting, I went out and the nurse said, "I want you to come with me. The doctor wants to talk to you." We went to a room and they had me sit down.

The doctor told me, "I'm afraid we have some bad news. It is cancer-embryonal cell corcisonenia, the second worse kind. I've already been to the library. We have one and one-half pages on this cancer, but I can tell you this, have you heard of Dr. Tom Dooley?"

"Yes sir, I've heard of him," I replied. I knew he was a missionary doctor to Laos.

Dr. Jerome said, "Well, they've just flown him to

the United States for treatment for the very same thing your husband has. Mrs. Sullivan, how do you think your husband will take this sort of news?"

I replied, "Of course, I know it will be very disturbing and very distressing, but I think with the help of our friends and family and the good Lord he can handle it."

The doctor continued, "Well, the reason I asked you is because I've had two different patients in less than a week that I've had to tell they had cancer and they both committed suicide."

"I don't think he will do that," I replied. Dr. Jerome continued, "Shall I tell him or do you want to tell him?" I said, "Doctor, you can explain it to him much better than I. I wish you would talk to him."

He continued, "You know we have to re-operate. He's going to have to have major surgery. I've got to follow all those lymph nodes. All the ones that might be infected have got to come out because that's where it spreads. He'll probably have to have some kind of radiation."

I didn't go home. I waited for the doctor to go in. They got Enoch and carried him out on the sun porch and the doctor told him what he had and what his chances were.

Dr. Jerome said, "I don't know, I won't say, I'm not the giver of life, but I can tell you that lots of people have what you have and live less that six months. You might have six months to six years, who knows? Lots of them live five years with all the treatment. I can't tell you how much time you've got, but I can tell you to go to you room tonight and pray."

Enoch replied, "Doctor, I've already prayed and

there'll be lots of other people praying."

It seemed that from the very beginning Enoch had a lot of faith that he would be all right. He went through the surgeries and he took 50 cobalt treatments. It was a very trying time for the family because when he stopped working, the income totally stopped except what the good people who saw and knew our needs provided for us. Our family was fed, our bills were met and it was because people cared about us. They cared about what we were going through and wanted to stand by us. I'll never forget it. Ministers and friends came and they brought groceries. That's the kind of love you never forget. It's like the love that should always be in the family of God as well as in our own families. Taking care of the needs of one another I think is part of the commandments. He said, "Love one another as I have loved you" and that's giving a whole lot when you give like the Lord does.

At the time of Enoch's illness our oldest son, Wayne, was ten years old and I was expecting our baby daughter, Lesa. People continued to pray and help in every way they could. Lesa was born April 1, 1961 and her presence seemed to give Enoch a new lease on life. As soon as I could, I went to work at Vanity Fair Mills and we continued our gospel singing on week-ends while Enoch was recovering from his ordeal.

The gospel work made more demands on us (radio programs, personal appearances and eventually T.V.) so I quit my job at the mill and we went into gospel work full time. Enoch continued to improve and has had regular check-ups for 25 years. Until this day he has not had a reoccurrence.

We are forever grateful to first of all, the Good Lord from whom all blessings flow and secondly to good people who helped us continue against the odds.

Doctors did what they could and the Lord took care of the rest. We must say He is the Great Physician. There is nothing too hard for Him to do.

Chapter 8

Bill Monroe and the Beginning
of the Bluegrass Festivals
Events from 1960 through 1969

ENOCH: We started 1960 off on a low note with me being diagnosed with cancer. It seemed like the end of the world, but the Lord has different ways of doing things and He always knows what he's doing and what He's doing is always best. Maybe I had cancer for Him to get our attention; to get us back down to earth again. It seemed very hopeless, but a lot came from that.

MARGIE: As soon as Enoch was able, we started back on the road and a lot of good doors opened for us. We continued to work radio programs. By then we had broadened to WSJC in Magee, MS which was a good 50,000-watt station and covered a big area. That helped us broaden out. We'd go to a place in Mississippi and there would be somebody there from Louisiana. They would invite us to Louisiana and the next thing we knew we were going to be in Texas, Arkansas, Florida, Georgia, Kentucky and Tennessee.

It just kept broadening. The opportunities to have radio programs and the opportunity to minister to big gatherings like camp meetings, conferences, conventions and things of that nature helped us meet more people and go more places.

In the early 1960's we continued on the road and new doors continued to open. The children were getting bigger and there was always school to reckon with. We had lot of baby-sitters who were committed to seeing to it the Sullivan Family continued. Some lived in our home; others just came and went. We always had competent people, along with Granny, who would help with the children and see that they were taken care of while we were on the road.

During the time of Enoch's illness, we met a man who had a profound impact on our lives - Mr. Walter Bailes. He was a member of the original Bailes Brothers, who used to be on the Grand Ole Opry and then the Louisiana Hayride on KWKH in Shreveport, LA in the 1930's, 40's and early 50's. That's where he met a minister who showed him the straight and narrow way. He was willing to accept it and walk in it and it changed his life forever.

He became a minister and the writer of many good songs like *Dust on the Bible, Give Mother my Crown, The Light in the Sky* and so many more. He still preaches at 79 years of age. He is very active in the ministry, still writes songs, has a program on WSM in Nashville, TN has television shows and a short wave radio ministry that reaches around the world. Our hats are off to you, Brother Walter.

Because of the calling on Brother Bailes' life and the inspiration the Lord gave him, he helped the Sullivan Family record a song in 1960 that became our first hit. It was called *Walking My Lord Up Calvary Hill.* We recorded for Brother Walter 14 years on Loyal Records. We had a lot of good songs during that time including *Working on a Building*, which was placed in the Library of Congress.

ENOCH: We met Brother Walter through a good preacher friend, Brother William Kemp. Brother Walter just loved our music. He heard about my cancer and was very concerned. He prayed for me and we formed a close friendship.

Brother Walter told us he wanted to start the Loyal Label and he wanted us to record string band style. At that time it wasn't called "bluegrass gospel." We recorded an extended play album, called an EP, which had four songs on it. In the studio were Emmett, Margie and myself and Jerry came in as a guest to help us. He sang and played bass. He was already working on a job and was not able to work full-time with us, so Patsy Jones played bass on some of the numbers. Frank Stuckey from Mobile, AL played rhythm guitar on that session. Our good preacher friend, Ernest Jones from Mobile, Patsy's father, was at the session with us.

The big number that came out of that session, of course, was *Walking My Lord Up Calvary Hill.* I was really weak and we had prayer in the studio for me to have the strength to do the song in the right way. It was aired just as soon as Brother Walter got it ready. He sent it to the 50,000-watt stations. The first 50,000-watt station to play it was WCKY in Cincinnati, OH and the disc jockey was our good friend, Wayne Raney. It immediately became the most requested song on that station. It didn't make any difference where we went, we could sing a whole concert, but the minute we sang that song, they knew who we were.

That was a highlight even to this day in our music business, because the first song that brings you national or international recognition is something you don't ever forget. It's hard to top it.

Brother Bailes did a lot for the Sullivan Family and he does a lot now. We try to always return the favors as much as we can. We've worked closely together all these years and we stand the same on just about everything.

MARGIE: We continued to write and learn new songs. Now and then a new song would be sent by the good Lord that was inspired and we would record those songs.

ENOCH: From childhood the first time I heard Bill and Charlie Monroe singing a duet, I knew I loved the mandolin and guitar playing better than just about anything I had heard before. The success of *Walking My Lord Up Calvary Hill* enabled us to meet people like Bill Monroe. I loved his music all my life. I loved his band and in 1960 he had a good one. He was not doing well financially because of rock and roll music. From 1954 when Elvis Presley rocked on the scene, it was hard times for people like Mr. Monroe, Roy Acuff and other true country music people.

We did so well with *Walking My Lord Up Calvary Hill*. Wilma Lee and Stoney Cooper recorded it earlier, but their recording of it didn't get off somehow or other. Stoney called to express how much he appreciated our recording it. He said he was really proud of us and proud for the lady who wrote the song, Ruby Moody of Knoxville, TN. She was a Christian lady and a very poor lady and Stoney said, "I'm more proud for her than anything else. Every time that song plays, it's helping a lady that I know needs and deserves the help."

I talked to Mr. Monroe early in the 1950's, but he wasn't interested in doing all gospel concerts then. In 1962 I decided I'd approach him again because we were drawing some good crowds on our own. I knew he needed to work, we all needed to work. I love him and his band and wanted to be friends with him and get to know him better. He was a hard man to get to know in those years. A lot of people didn't understand him, I could tell that. I'd done a lot of emceeing and learned a lot about the nature of people.

Emmett and I went to the Grand Ole Opry at the old Ryman Auditorium to see him again and see what we could do. There was a disc jockey convention going on in Nashville. We forgot to go over to the radio station in Mobile and get our passes to go backstage at the Opry. We found out we were better known than we thought we were. When we got there the backstage guard, J. D. Bell, wanted to know about our passes.

I told him, "We didn't bring them, but we're the Sullivan Family from the station in Mobile with Mr. Jack Cardwell and Boots Barnes." Mr. Barnes was a policeman and disc jockey and the one who started the show *Backstage at the Opry*. He'd go to the Opry and record and bring the recordings back to Mobile and play for the country fans. They named the segment *Backstage at Grand Ole Opry with Boots Barnes*. When I mentioned Mr. Barnes, Mr. Bell stated, "Oh yes, that'll be all right. You don't have to have the passes, you come on in." So I guess we got in "illegally" at the Opry in 1962.

Wilma Lee and Stoney Cooper were popular back then, as was Joe Stuart, who said, "You all come on and let's go back to Bill's dressing room right now." That was the first time backstage for us and on the way back we ran into Carl and Pearl Butler who had the number one hit *Don't Let Me Cross Over*. Everybody was just hugging them and Joe Stuart brought us around to where they were and there was a "big huggin' and carryin' on." While we were talking to them, Patsy Cline came to congratulate them on their hit. When she got there, Jim Reeves also congratulated them. We were just standing there and I guess back then everybody thought we were "outstanding lookin' fellows." There Emmett and I were, both with a black head of hair, tall, dressed up in our Sunday best and each sporting a little mustache, which nobody had back then except Stoney Cooper.

When Patsy Cline got there, there were a lot of country music and news people who wanted to take pictures. They said to Patsy, "We want your picture too, come here, come here." She replied, "I'll let you take my picture if you will let me have these two good looking men on each side of me." She caught us around the shoulders; me on one side and Emmett on the other. They took the pictures. I would love to have a copy of one of those pictures.

After we got to see Mr. Monroe, I approached him again about work. I told him I had some good contacts in Louisiana, Mississippi, Arkansas and Alabama and I thought we could have some good concerts and draw some good crowds.

He said, "I don't know. I do an awful lot of gospel singing, but I'm just a little bit afraid to do it. You see, I've sung *Footprints In The Snow, Uncle Pen, Muleskinner Blues and Blue Moon of Kentucky* so long I believe the people will demand me to sing them even on an all gospel program."

I said, "No sir, we couldn't do that. A lot of these preachers and people that are going to back us are fundamentalists and are real strict. They believe worldly music doesn't have any place in church. They call worldly music 'sinful music.'"

Mr. Monroe spoke up with heavy concern in his voice, "Mr. Sullivan I never done any bad songs. I've given up songs that made hits which had the word 'whiskey' in them and vulgar talk. I wouldn't record them. I've never recorded anything but straight working music, family music and real to life music. I don't do any bad songs. In fact I've got a preacher in Virginia that gets up on the stage and plays the mandolin and sings *Muleskinner Blues* with me."

"Yes sir, I know that," I replied, "but it won't work down South with the people we're going to be working with."

Mr. Monroe said, "Well, I'm afraid they'll ask for

86

my other songs." I told him, "No sir, I guarantee you they won't. I'm going to emcee the program and I'll set the stage to where it would be out of order for them to ask for anything but a religious song." He said he would think about it.

Not too long after that, Mr. Monroe came to Grove Hill, AL about 30 miles from our place. I'll have to interject here that some booking agents can be very careless with the way they book artists. Some just don't understand. This particular man booked Mr. Monroe into an armory. When Mr. Monroe got to the armory, there was no crowd. The promotion had not been done. He played a few tunes and the promoter told him that we would go down to Jackson, AL and he thought he could get a crowd down there. This was happening all during the same evening.

We got down to Jackson and there was no crowd. The promoter couldn't even get the place open, couldn't unlock it. He said, "Let's go on down to Chickasaw, AL another 60 miles down the road and by this time it was getting late at night. I went on with them because I felt concern. The promoter called ahead and when we got there, he couldn't get any chairs for the place. It didn't make any difference anyway because there was nobody there either. It was hard times.

Some of the Masonic people came around and said they had a friend in Pascagoula, MS who had a club and he said if Mr. Bill didn't mind playing in a club, they'd have a crowd and they'd go all night. They went on and I went back home. Before he left, Mr. Monroe told me to call him the following Monday that he had some open dates. He called Margie and gave her the dates and she booked a tour down to the edge of the coast and back to our area in Jackson.

The first date was in Bond School, just out of

Philadelphia, MS. It was packed out and running over. We went on to Baton Rouge, Albany, Pearl River and Bogalusa in Louisiana, Picayune, MS and ended up back at Fulton, AL, a sawmill and logging community just north of Jackson. Every one of the shows was packed.

I was always concerned for people who carried a band. It is a big responsibility and I always hoped they would make enough money. Mr. Bill and his band had to stay in motels back then and they were traveling in an old brown Oldsmobile station wagon that didn't even have reverse in it.

I knew it was costing him, but he told me, "Mr. Sullivan, working like this if I can make as much as $100 a night and then go back and work the Opry on the weekend, I'll be all right.

I remember as hard as I worked approaching him in the 1950's and again in early 1962, that it was so hard to get things arranged and get the okay from him. To our knowledge it was the first shows he ever did billed as "string band gospel concerts." We did a series of three in 1962, 1963 and 1964 and every time they were successful.

We were getting acquainted with Mr. Monroe and becoming great friends. After the first tour he called me right back, saying he thought they turned out good and we should do some more and "could we rig 'em up?"

In the mid-1960's, just after we'd done the concerts with Mr. Monroe, I heard him on WSM with Grant Turner on the *Opry Warm-Up Show*. We were on our way to Louisiana and listening to the Nashville station. Grant was doing an interview will Mr. Monroe and he informed him that from that night forward his music would be called "Bluegrass Music." Grant replied, "Yes, that's right Bill. Your band is the Bluegrass Boys, you're from Kentucky which is the 'Bluegrass State' and your music is bluegrass, but you'll be doing country music on the Grand Ole Opry."

"No, I don't want my music to be referred to as country music any more," Bill told him. "I want to separate my music from country music. It's now bluegrass."

Grant asked, "Well, you're going to stay on the Opry?" Bill replied, "There ain't nothing changing. I just want a separation in the music. I can identify my music as 'bluegrass music.' The reason I'm doing that is I'm not exactly pleased with the way country music is going right now."

That was all the explanation Mr. Bill gave Grant. I pulled over and parked the car cause it concerned all of us. I was always trying to gain ground for the bluegrass gospel music. I said, "Well, it looks like now they're going to get into it and they're going to have a falling out and they'll fire Bill off the Grand Ole Opry. That winds up all the ground we've gained. We'll have to start all over again."

But they talked it out and they didn't have a misunderstanding. They had an understanding, but it was strict. Anytime Grant Turner played a Bill Monroe record, he would say, "This is a Bill Monroe with the sound of bluegrass music." That's when bluegrass music was named. Bill Monroe's music officially became 'bluegrass,' named by him.

The country music business was having a hard time. Carlton Haney, a promoter from Virginia, decided in 1965 that he would put together 'homecoming' and 'get-together' shows. They didn't know what to call it, he just said, "We'll have a big festival, a big festivity. We won't invite nobody but string bands, mountain music."

Hootenanny music had come out with the long neck banjos. It was kind of like jazz and country. None of our people were going to go with that because it was too much like 'folk music.' We had just had a downfall with Elvis Presley's rock and roll coming on the scene. Now here came the hippies with their hootenanny and that was tearing up the string band music.

So they were going to have one more big ole mountain music revival or reunion or get-together. The arrangements were made for Labor Day weekend at Watermelon Park at Berryville, VA. The show was composed of Bill Monroe, Ralph Stanley, Jim and Jesse, the Osborne Brothers and Don Reno and Red Smiley. And everybody in the world who played bluegrass and could hear about the show came to it. They thought it was going to be the last 'get-together,' but it proved to be the start - the very first festival. At the same time they had a festival at Woodstock, NY, which featured rock music. It got out of hand, according to country peoples' standards and many were very displeased.

Mr. Monroe saw from his first bluegrass festival in Bean Blossom, IN in 1966 that there was a spillover from Woodstock and he wanted to make a distinction between a rock festival and a bluegrass festival. Bluegrass was and is a working man's music - Christian, gospel and God-fearing. That's how we got the job.

When Mr. Monroe asked me, he said, "I want you to be on my festival and come to Bean Blossom and help me." I remember saying, "Mr. Bill, I don't know how I could help you." I was thinking in terms of music.

He replied, "No, I'm not talking about music, but

you can help me that way, too. I've traveled down South with you and doing concerts with you and I realize the fact that the ministers down there and all them church people trust you all. If I advertise that you're going to be at my festival, it'll let people know that God-fearing people come to my festival; the people that go to church every Sunday and read their Bible. People that believe in God will know that we are having a family festival. We're going to have a church service every Sunday and I want you to help me with the hymn singing."

That's what we always did for Mr. Monroe. All the people that were on stage Saturday, he wanted them to stay over for the Sunday morning service. He would open the service and call all the bands to come up on stage with him. He wanted everybody to wear their coats and have their best on for Sunday. He wanted each group as a band, but all together as a choir. We'd start singing. He loved to sing *I Saw The Light* and *I'll Fly Away* and maybe he'd call on Ralph Stanley and his band to lead a song like *You've Got To Walk That Lonesome Valley*. He'd call us around to do *Just A Little Talk With Jesus Makes It Right*. We'd sing as a bluegrass choir for maybe 30 minutes and then he'd introduce the preacher, who would do just a regular Sunday morning service. Then he'd call the bands around and we'd play something like *Pass Me Not* and he's take up an offering for the preacher. Then he'd call on somebody to close in prayer.

On Sunday afternoon and evening, they'd go back to regular bluegrass, but we'd always do the hymn singing on Sunday morning. That was a highlight of our life.

I never quite saw the reception like we got that first time in 1968. We went up early and played some of the churches in the area and invited them to come and be with us on Sunday and they all came. There was Emmett, Margie and myself, and I think Jerry on bass and Lambert Areno on dobro. Lambert was from Sulphur, LA and had played with Walter Bailes and Johnny and Jack. He was a Cajun and a good one.

A lot of great bands in bluegrass today would not understand what I'm talking about because that was so long ago. Everybody that was in bluegrass was in it right there. I remember Don Reno and Red Smiley, who was so sick at the time, and Red Allen from Harlan, KY was there. He was very prominent in bluegrass and had recorded with the Osborne Brothers. He was an authority on bluegrass. Then there was Bill Harrell and Buck Ryan, who was a world champion fiddler who played with Jimmy Dean. He was a master fiddler and hailed from New York.

When we did our all gospel program, it meant a lot to me and I'll never forget it. Margie started off with *Matthew Twenty-Four*. We had just recorded *Old Brush Arbor By The Side of the Road*. Shot Jackson had played dobro on the record, so we had Lambert Areno with us to take the same breaks. When we did that song, and church people will understand what I'm talking about, the spirit of the Lord came in a special, special way. Most anybody would understand that. You just have a visit from a higher power that came there to be with us. I don't think you could have found a man or woman who wasn't crying. Audibly you could hear people crying all over the place and you could see their tears.

We came out the back door of the old Brown County Jamboree, it was an old milking barn, and standing in the middle of the doorway, the first man to catch me was Don Reno. He said, "That's the most powerful singing I've every heard. That's better than the days of Molly O'Day or anybody else." Molly O'Day was the spiritual factor in their lives. Don said, "I've never felt like this. I want you to do my songs and help me. I want to let you know that I'm with you and I haven't heard anything like than in years."

The next man that caught and embraced me was Ralph Stanley. His singing partner and brother, Carter, had just died. Ralph said, "I don't know whether or not I should continue in the music business without Carter. There were tears in his eyes and I said, "Yeah Ralph, you've got to go on. You can't stop. You were part of it too. Carter's gone, but the people love both of you. We'll always love Carter, but we love you and the people do too and you just get up there and get in there."

I feel like Ralph took hope to go on and considered what I was saying. He said, "Yes, maybe that's the best thing I can do." I replied, "That's all you can do. There are other boys who can sing that part. After all, you are the tenor and tenor plays a great part in your kind of singing. Your voice is what set it aside and made it just a little bit different."

That same year we played Ralph Stanley's festival in McClure, VA and it was there we met the Osborne Brothers. They'd had a show the day before and they stayed over to meet us. They had heard our song *I'll Meet You In Church Sunday Morning*. A preacher's son from Florida was working with them and he said, "Yes, I know those people real well, the Sullivan Family, you going to see them at Ralph's." Sonny Osborne told them he was in no hurry to leave and he'd stay right there until he met us. Sonny's a very honest, straightforward man who means what he says and says what he means. The Osborne Brothers, Jim and Jesse and Mac Wiseman are some of the greatest people in bluegrass music.

Right after Bill's second festival, he said to me, "Let's set up some more of these." This was a great day for the Sullivan Family. If you had come from where I had, starting before it was called bluegrass and if you loved the music as much as I, and seeing it have a hard time getting to where it was - it getting to you and you getting to it; then it was such a marvelous day for us when Mr. Monroe said, "Let's set up some more." He was a man that was on the Grand Ole Opry and in a position to do that and put it across and we were right by his side.

Mr. Bill opened a festival in Jackson, KY and one in Cosby, TN, which he gave to his son, James Monroe.

He told me to set up one in Alabama. We did it in my home county, Washington, and it was known as Lockwood Park. The probate judge and other elected officials brought it in. I introduced the program to them with Mr. Carl Story. He went to the courthouse with me to get a proclamation for it. We started the festival and it was highly successful.

It was the highlight in our lives to have people in the country come by and say, "I didn't think that I would ever get to see Bill Monroe and you brought him right out here in these woods." The park was five miles from the nearest telephone or electric line. Jack Edwards, who was our Congressman, told the REA to get the current to us as quickly as possible. They brought in the power trucks and they put the lines up and it was a big time for Washington County.

Then we went down to Louisiana and got a proclamation from Gov. John J. McKeithen and we put one at Walker, LA at the Old South Jamboree with my good friend Lester Hodges.

Then we went to McKinney, TX and had a festival on a 50-acre farm. Tudy Williams ran that one for Bill. When we put the one in at Lockwood, Bill said, "Now that's going to be the Sullivan Family and Bluegrass Boys' Festival." He gave everything it made to his band and the Sullivan Family. He did as much for the Sullivan Family and me as he did for his own band and son. He treated us just as good. He said, "This will be yours and you'll work hard on it and I'll be right here to help you and bring the people down here to make it go." We all got the same treatment.

In 1993, Mr. Bill placed us in his Bluegrass Hall of Fame. In doing so he gave us equal billing with his son, members of his band and his co-workers like Mac Wiseman and all the greats in bluegrass. He gave us the same position he did them and I'll be forever grateful to him for as long as I live because a man can't give you any more than that.

You say, "Well, what about Bill Monroe?" He was peculiar to some people and as I said he was hard to know. People never did understand him, but as Marge will tell you, and she is a minister, as the years would roll by I saw him change from one personality to another. He changed into a different man. He got to be one of the kindest (he was always kind), and one of the most considerate men I've known. He was kind, but he was strict. I heard him get on stage at a Festival in Apoka, FL with Brother R.L. Thorne, a powerful, spirit filled and very outstanding minister, and tell him, "Brother Thorne, I'm so glad I'm here. This is wonderful. I can feel the spirit of the Lord here in a great way."

MARGIE: He had a great respect for ministers. The only way you could tear that down was by bad conduct. He could lose respect for people, but I'm so proud to say that he never lost his respect for us. There were things that he asked us to do that I would never put into words because it was of a confidential nature and personal things that he needed to have done and he trusted us to do for him.

ENOCH: I remember telling Emmett and Marge

95

all the time that the string band music was going to do as good as the rest of it; that it had a place. We had country, southern gospel and classical gospel with people like George Beverly Shea, but there was no rock or contemporary gospel at that time.

At the festivals in Louisiana in 1968 and 69, Mr. Bill asked me, "Have you all ever thought about calling yourselves the Sullivan Brothers? There's a lot of brother acts." I know he was thinking about himself and his brother, Charlie.

I said, "Yes I know, but Margie sings in the group too and I guess we'll always stay the Sullivan Family." He replied, "Well, why don't you call your singing bluegrass gospel? You use the same approach to music that I use. Why don't you just call yours bluegrass gospel? That would be fine with me."

He named our music bluegrass gospel. We didn't classify it, we let Bill Monroe, the founder and "King of Bluegrass Music," do it for us.

We had a lot of help from the musicians in southern gospel. Mr. J. G. Whitfield, who was known as "The Old Gospel Man," had a program on WEAR-TV in Pensacola, FL. Mr. Whitfield's "Pleasing Food Stores" sponsored it. He invited the Sullivan Family to come and be on the television program and play Bonifey, FL, the biggest all night gospel singing in the world. It was located at the football stadium.

They had just moved the Southern Gospel Convention from Memphis, TN to Nashville, TN. It was the 25th anniversary that Mr. Whitfield invited us to appear on it. We were the first and only bluegrass gospel group that had done that, I believe, until the last two or three years when they had the Isaacs and Doyle Lawson and Quicksilver.

Joel and Labreeska Hemphill are just like family to us. Joel's dad, Rev. W.T. Hemphill, was Margie's pastor at different times. We met the original Chuck Wagon Gang, Roy Carter and his sisters Rose and Anna; Jimmie Davis, former Louisiana Governor; Les Beasley and the Florida Boys, the Blackwood Brothers and the Statesmen. We had great respect for all those folks and we couldn't lose. We had some of the greatest friends on earth pulling for us in bluegrass. Of course, there was Bill Monroe, Ralph Stanley and Jim and Jesse McReynolds. Then there was Roy Acuff, Walter Bailes and the Bailes Brothers, Charlie Louvin, Carl and Pearl Butler and people like that in the country field were pulling hard for us. They wouldn't stop until they got the disc jockey to know that they needed to play some of our music. Disc jockeys like Jack Cardwell, I call him our hometown DJ from Mobile, AL was pulling for us. Jack was an honorable man and a Baptist minister. We knew him before he was converted and he later became a pastor for a church. He was the greatest personality to ever be in Mobile.

With all those people pulling for you, how could you miss? That was some of the happiest times of my life when we would all meet maybe at Bean Blossom and play and go on traveling in busses and cars. It would be Bill Monroe, Ralph Stanley, Lester Flatt, Jim and Jesse, the Osborne Brothers, Mac Wiseman and James Monroe. We'd all maybe leave Indiana and drive into Virginia. We'd all drive along together and we'd stop at a café and it would just turn the place upside down. A lot of times we'd be traveling in the morning and Mr. Bill would want to stop and get breakfast and he would pay for everybody. It seemed that everyone in bluegrass was in that group back then. When we'd leave one another, we'd maybe say, "We'll see you in McKinney, TX" and everybody would meet there next. I remember Jim Brock was the fiddler for Jim and Jesse and he lived in Hamilton, AL. He'd catch our bus and maybe go to Florida and work with them and then catch us back home. It was a great time. Most everybody affectionately called Bill "Dad." We all looked up to him. We'd all get together on his birthday and buy him a new suit or something.

MARGIE: Two wonderful things happened to me in the 1960's. The United Pentecostal Church in New Orleans, LA when Brother Boyce Dunn was the pastor, bought me a D18 Martin guitar, which I still use. It had hung on the wall of a music store for several years and I don't know why they felt that inclination, but they did. They presented it from the rostrum of their church at a time when we were playing down there.

Then in the '60's we were playing a remote broadcast for Boots Barnes and one of the stations in Mobile. It was a hot, hot day and the bridge came off my guitar. I made the statement, "I don't know what in the world I'm going to do for a guitar until I get this one fixed." Boots said, "Miss Margie, I've got an old D28 at home under the bed that George Morgan gave me. If it'll be any help to you, I'll go get it. It needs new strings." He loaned it to me and as it turned out he was ready to trade it in on a new one. I told him to find out what they would give him for a trade-in on it and I wanted to buy it. I'm almost ashamed to tell you what I paid for it. It was $200 for the guitar and case. It's the guitar George Morgan used when he recorded the big hit *Candy Kisses* back in 1949 and he also used it on the Grand Ole Opry and on his tours around the world.

During the 1960's we worked in different political campaigns. Hon. George C. Wallace was our governor and he contacted us and we worked some tours with him. He'd have Hank Williams Jr. and us and different ones from the Opry. We went with him to rallies throughout Alabama. We also worked for Mrs. Lurlene Wallace, his wife, when she ran for governor. She was one of the greatest ladies we ever knew. She did not get to serve her full term. She died of cancer.

We went to her wake in Montgomery. She weighed only 68 pounds. I have thought so much about how good the Lord was to heal Enoch of cancer and yet the governor of our state was not spared. My only conclusion is that the Lord knows best for everyone.

We worked a lot of campaigns in Mississippi for Jimmy Swan. We temporarily moved our headquarters to WBKH radio in Hattiesburg, MS. They provided us a mobile home and we had daily syndicated radio broadcasts throughout the state. The secretaries at the station would keep our children so we could go almost every night for 18 months to introduce Jimmy Swan to over 400 church groups in the state.

We played every county seat at least three times. There are 82 counties in Mississippi. Sometimes we would play five or six times a day during the campaign. We could set up in three minutes, play 15 minutes and take down in three minutes and be on to our next stop.

Back then you had a caravan with a sound crew, a truck and people who gave out bumper stickers and other campaign literature. They called it stump speaking back then. The candidates usually had a band to help draw a crowd. I don't guess they do it anywhere any more. We usually set up in front of the courthouses. The candidates wanted to meet the people and shake their hands and get to know them on a personal basis. Now television has taken all that away.

In 1966 Jerry Sullivan, Enoch's uncle, left his job at a chemical plant and came to work with us on the bass fiddle. I rented he and Emmett each a place to stay. We all moved to Hattiesburg, MS and stayed until 1967 and then went back again in 1971 to help Jimmy.

In 1968 while there, we gained in publicity and popularity. We made some more recordings for Walter Bailes. Jimmy Swan produced *Sing Daddy A Song* through his radio station and it became a hit. Jimmy was a charter member of the Country Music Disc Jockey Association and he had the contacts to put that song across for us. Jerry wrote the song in memory of my daddy, the Rev. Arthur Sullivan. *Light in the Sky* was a good one for us, too.

Chapter 9

Radio, T.V., and Festivals from Alabama to Canada
The Decade of the 1970's

ENOCH: In the 1970's we did a live recording. We spoke about B. J. Johnson from WRJW in Picayune, MS, where we first started. He was still disc jockeying and had a studio. We got a chance to make a live recording and called it *The Philadelphia, Mississippi Homecoming.*

A lot of good things happened for us in Philadelphia. That's the first town in which I ever emceed a program many years prior to the recording. I remember in the early 1970's is when we added to the band. The band consisted of Margie, Emmett and myself and we had three young fellows join. Marty Stuart from Philadelphia, MS was 12 and played the mandolin and fiddle. Carl Jackson from Louisville, MS came to us from Jim and Jesse and he played flat top guitar and also swapped out and played some banjo and he and Emmett played some twin banjos on some recordings. We also had a young fellow from Pine Bluff, AK named Ronnie Dickerson who played bass, but he was also a good guitar, dobro and mandolin player. He was very talented. These three youngsters worked with us from 1970-71.

MARGIE: We had our own television shows from Channel 12, Channel 16 and Channel 3 TV in Jackson, MS sponsored by Ford Motor Co. and General Electric. They were very successful and received high ratings. We taped once a month and did four shows at a time. We had many guests including Brock Speer and the Speer Family, Carl Story and the Rambling Mountaineers, Carl and Pearl Butler, James Monroe and the Midnight Ramblers and others. We were fortunate in that Enoch looked ahead and saw that we needed to save the film. That footage is very, very important now as a history of those years, not only for us, but also for the other groups who appeared as well.

The television shows opened many doors for us to sing and play. People instantly knew who we were. You could be on television tonight and tomorrow everybody in town knew who you were.

ENOCH: I remember too Margie, during the late 1960's and early '70, we were able to bring in a lot of festivals. A lot of people would come and pick out places they thought would be good for a festival. We helped Dickie Alexander with the Red River Festival near Coushatta, LA, Johnny Martin of LaPorte, TX with a festival at Pitkin, LA and Clyde Baum's Festival at Pollock, LA. We brought in festivals that were good for Mississippi at the time. It started out from Hattiesburg, to Runnelstown, to Decatur, to Raleigh and back down to Wiggins, where it's held now. We produced the one at Wiggins, along with Bill Monroe until he got too busy with his work schedule. He turned it over to us and we, along with A. R. Byrd, have continued the festival. A lot of that type thing came from our television shows.

And in 1976 we went to Canada. The Shriners invited us to a festival there and we crossed the border at Houlton, Maine.

The band included Emmett on banjo, Marge on guitar, Richard Alexander on the bass and helping drive the bus and me on fiddle. On that trip we also played the Strawberry Festival at Woodstock, New Brunswick, Canada, which is considered "the Woodstock in Canada." It was on this trip Margie wrote her signature song for her native state, *Name A Spot in Heaven Louisiana.*

On July 19, 1976 we made our first appearance on the Grand Ole Opry. I'll never forget it. In that same year we went to Nova Scotia and took our music to Canada. We'd never done that before.

Shot Jackson, a musician in Nashville who used to play the steel guitar and dobro with the Bailes Brothers, Johnny and Jack and Roy Acuff and who also found Sho-Bud Guitar Co., brought about releasing a double album for us in Canada and it sold real good. It was really great to tour that country and have our own recording company there where people could buy our material. We've made three tours in Canada.

We recorded some songs in the 1970's with Walter Bailes that were really good for us. *What A Wonderful Savior Is He* was probably the most popular.

ENOCH: *Bluegrass Unlimited*, the voice of bluegrass music, did a cover story on us in the October 1980 issue. It featured a picture of us on the cover and a five-page story with seven pictures. It was really nice.

MARGIE: The magazine also rated *What A Wonderful Savior Is He* with four stars and said it was the best, by far, bluegrass gospel album that had been recorded that year.

We recorded *The Gospel Train* and *Working On A Building*. The United States Library of Congress requested a copy for their archives for the history of music. That was a very high honor.

In the 1970's they came out with the Splato Festivals. We were privileged to be booked at the Brooklyn, NY Academy of Music on two different occasions by our late and great friend, Kathy Kaplin, who was a radio announcer in New York. She helped to head up the committee choosing the talent for the Splato Festivals. One of the festivals was held in Charleston, SC and was televised via satellite around the world.

ENOCH: One very great friend who did a wonderful job with us in every phase was Bob Burnham, who was a retired Navy man from Hattiesburg, MS. He was a good bus driver, mechanic, bass player and singer. He worked with us a lot off and on and he was ready to go anytime. Sometime Joe Stuart was there and sometime Jerry was there. We would put Jerry on the flat top and Bob would play bass. We had a strong band.

MARGIE: In 1977 we had a bad wreck. We were awhile getting over it. That made a change in our schedule. It was two months before I could travel. I really wasn't up to it, but I wanted to and I did. I was in a walker and in a cast, but felt it was necessary to make myself go back to work.

ENOCH: One of the highlights was our first program after the wreck. It was at Rebel Park near Marthaville, LA, built by our great friend Mr. Robert Gentry. He's written a two volume set about the history of KWKH's Louisiana Hayride and he's the one who has brought about the writing of this book about us. Prior to this there were two people who wrote about the Sullivan Family. Mr. Charles Burns of Mt. Vernon, AL attempted to write the first story. Bob Cagle of Bethel Springs, TN did a lot of work. Both of them got disabled before they got the books done, but they were very instrumental in keeping up with our history.

Anyway, back to my story. Our first appearance after the wreck was at Rebel Park with Ernest Tubb, Wilma Lee and Stoney Cooper and a lot of people from the Grand Ole Opry. Carl Jackson was there with us on guitar.

MARGIE: I know I remember one thing. Enoch told me to call and cancel. We'd had the wreck in March and I was on the walker for 11 months. I had graduated from the bed to the walker in May. I had really wanted to do this date because Mr. Gentry set it up. It was a real important program and it had a lot of important people there, including the governor of Louisiana, Edwin W. Edwards, as special guest. He had been a friend of ours and also Mr. Gentry's. Since I was doing so poorly, Enoch said, "Now Margie, I mean, when I come back in from work today, I want you to cancel that date. You're not able to go and I think it's too early for you to go back out and work the road."

I called Mr. Gentry with the full intention of canceling the date. When I got him on the phone, he didn't know about the wreck or how badly I was hurt. The first thing, in a good bubbly, excited voice, he said, "Oh guess where you will be playing? I'm putting you on just before Gov. Edwards comes on."

I said, "Oh, is that right?" When I heard that, I knew that he'd had the programs printed and everything else. So I said, "Well, I called to find out what time we would play and also, I wanted to know if you could provide me with a stool. I will need it to sit down while I play." I still didn't go into any details about the wreck.

When we got to Rebel Park, you talk about three people - Enoch, Emmett and myself - who looked like they'd been run over by a stalk cutter, we did. Carl Jackson met us there and some of the Areno Boys from Sulphur, LA and others joined in to help us on the program. I'll never forget how happy I felt to know that we made that first date and that I was able to do it. Still there was speculation and people saying, "Why don't you let her get well?"

My doctor told Enoch, "She'll get well if you'll take her out there where the people are and where she's used to working. She's not ever going to get well, she'll just worry herself to death at home, so take her on out there, that's the best therapy that she can have." It proved to be true - people helped me to get well. There really should be a chapter about Mr. Gentry in this book. He's a great man in every sense of the word. He helped to keep the history of country, bluegrass and bluegrass gospel music straight. He's collected many different artifacts and memorabilia and has them displayed in The Robert Gentry Museum in Many, LA. When you are in the area, be sure and go by for a visit. You'll find memorabilia from the Sullivan Family there. Look for the big building that looks like The Alamo on San Antonio Ave. in downtown Many.

Billie Jean Horton was at Rebel Park that day, May 13, 1977 and she presented Mr. Gentry with some things from Hank Williams Sr.'s life. She had been married to him for three months before his death. She later married Johnny Horton and he was killed in a car wreck. She brought things from both of these famous stars and presented to Mr. Gentry for the museum for country music.

Mr. Gentry was always and still is very active in country music. He was a great friend of Roy Acuff's and so many other of the stars. I remember on one occasion, he journeyed to Nashville, TN and made a presentation to Mr. Acuff on the Opry. He also did the same thing for Charlie Louvin, who is one of his dear friends. He has many, many friends among the country people. To think that he thought enough of the Sullivan Family that he wanted to write about our life makes us humble and grateful for a friend like him.

ENOCH: One of the reasons he was so instrumental in all of this is he learned about country music early on from the Louisiana Hayride in Shreveport in the 1940's and on through the '60's. The Hayride was like the Cass Walker Show in Knoxville, TN. It was a stepping stone to the Opry. County music people would go to the Hayride and if they kicked off real good and made a hit and went over big, then they'd head for the Opry. Then again, sometimes there would be people at the Opry who could come to Shreveport because it was a good outlet for country music.

MARGIE: I remember Mr. Charlie Monroe came down and spent a long session at KWKH. In fact, I heard more bluegrass and bluegrass gospel on KWKH than I ever heard on WSM. At one time Mac Wiseman was there, along with the Bailes Brothers, Charlie Monroe and the Kentucky Partners, Clyde Baum and his Bayou Boys, Jimmy Martin and the Sunny Mountain Boys and Buzz Busby and his band. Clyde Baum was a good friend and later had his festivals at Shady Dell Park near Pollock, LA. He also worked with Bill Monroe. Johnny and Jack and Kitty Wells were also at KWKH. Mr. Gentry knows a lot about this because he has followed it. He knows a lot about the Sullivan Family because he's followed our career for many years and has been a true friend. He also knows the many friends we have made, especially in Louisiana, among country and bluegrass music people and a lot of the politicians.

In 1978 and '79, our plans were coming together to kick off an overseas tour in Europe, Holland and Belgium.

ENOCH: In late 1979 or early '80, James Philips, who played mandolin with us for many years and stood by us in all the recordings, was trying to retire. He told us we ought to hire 'Little Joe Cook' to help us on the mandolin and go when he couldn't.

Little Joe's first professional appearance was at Bill Monroe's Festival at Bean Blossom, IN. He was young and on the way up there we stopped at a rest area to get ready. Joe was only about 13, but he carried his shaving kit and everything. It was real fun to watch him lather his face to shave. I believe it was Paul MaHarrey who took his finger, raked it across his face to shave him and told Joe all he needed was a cat to lick that lather off. Joe didn't have any whiskers, but he was going to shave like all the big men.

The personnel of the band changed about this time. Paul MaHarrey knew he wouldn't be making the trip to Holland with us, so he and Emmett were teaching our daughter, Lesa, the bass. Vicki Cook, Joe's sister, was working on the guitar, flat-picking and finger picking. She was also a good banjo picker, being taught by Carl Jackson. It was the beginning of the troop we took to Holland with us in 1979.

MARGIE: You're talking about a trip. For us older folks with three teenagers on the bus, that was a trip. Everybody needed to be a part of that! They had fun all the time.

ENOCH: I always said it like this, "When you got young people with you on the road, they're troopin' with you and they turn out to be real troopers, but there's something about young people. They always got something going when you want it-and a lot of times, they go something going when you don't want it. But there's always something going."

MARGIE: I remember one time Emmett had bought a new pair of boots. The kids would get in the back of the bus, where they could close the door and lock it where the driver, who was usually Enoch or Emmett, couldn't tell what was going on. You always knew something was going on. They got back there and they got to pillow fighting. I think they tore up every pillow we had on the bus. Of course some of them were feather pillows and you can imagine how many feathers went flying.

ENOCH: When they ran out of pillows, they started using shoes and boots. As we said, Emmett had a new pair of patent leather boots, pretty, classy boots. Our daughter, Lesa, ran out of pillows to throw at Little Joe, so she threw one of Emmett's boots. It hit him, glanced off and went out the window and we lost a boot. He never even got a chance to wear them. They were scared to tell us. If they had told us, we would have stopped to get it. So, Emmett went to hunting his boots and he only had one.

MARGIE: They always played a lot of tricks on everybody. We girls would go back to our beds and turn in and leave the driving to the men. They always concocted ways to scare us. They weren't happy unless they could scare us. Enoch instigated just about everything. Little Joe would sit up in the front with him and Emmett. Emmett was a prankster from the word go.

We had the emergency brake catch on fire once and we all had to bail out and throw sand on it to put the fire out. It almost burned up. They would set us up for these pranks before we went to bed. They would say, "Remember that time the bus caught on fire? That would be bad for the bus to catch on fire and for us to lose our good instruments and clothes and all."

At this particular time we had a metal trash basket on the bus and Enoch told Joe, "I want you to get that metal trash basket, put some toilet paper in it, start a fire and smother it out so it smokes. Then you run to the back of the bus hollering 'fire' and let's see what these girls do."

There was a milk jug full of water back there and

when they went to hollering 'fire,' I grabbed the milk jug, Vicki grabbed her guitar and Lesa just grabbed at me. We all make a run for the door.

ENOCH: We were out on a long dark stretch just between Pine Bluff, AK and Lake Village, AK where it's the most desolate country in the world, not a light to be seen and it was a dark and cloudy night. I just pulled over right quick and they all bailed out there in the black of night.

MARGIE: And they all went to laughing.

ENOCH: There was Margie with that gallon of water to put out the fire.

MARGIE: Well, you always carry your weapon, be it big or small. I'll tell you one thing, we had a lot of fun and enjoyed the years the young folks worked with us. We carried them to Europe with us and it was like a working vacation.

ENOCH: They would be like family to us and I know Little Joe loved me like his own dad. I guess there couldn't have been a greater gift for us than to have those young folks working with us. I think they enjoyed it. I know they sometime got awful homesick. But when Little Joe married Kim Myers, they got to go to Holland with us on their honeymoon. I was thinking how much different that was from how Marge and me spent our honeymoon.

MARGIE: Well, I never had one and you know we've been married 50 years and I think it's about time we have one. I really didn't know what a honeymoon was when we got married. I didn't know exactly what that meant. All it ever meant to me was a whole lot of hard work.

ENOCH: Mostly what we were acquainted with

was honey buns.

MARGIE: And a pint of milk.

From the 1970's to the '80's was good. We did some recording and we did some things that I think were very beneficial to the furtherance of bluegrass gospel music.

That was always our aim and I remember an illustration you made one time. Everybody knows we've always done gospel music. We always felt bluegrass gospel music had a message in it. Many times, like when in Poland or overseas, we couldn't really testify or preach, but we could sing the word of God in the songs. So I really think we used it like you said a spider uses its web. We'd steer them in with the music and then we'd preach to them and tell them what they needed. It was always our goal for it to be more than just entertainment.

ENOCH: I was always happy that our music did attract good people. Little Marty Stuart said one time that the Sullivan Family's music seemed to attract good people. I always wanted to do that and reach out to people. The late Jack Cardwell, a Baptist minister, said, "Your music is an honest music. You can tell it's honest and has an honest approach to the people. It breeds honesty and what you're doing is good for the country."

I like to feel that way about it. I think with that band in the years of the '70's and '80's was a good time. The years as they roll by just get better and better. Of course, we all are getting older and older, but we are also getting better and better. We always look forward to the next season or the next series of recordings and try to stay on track as much as we can.

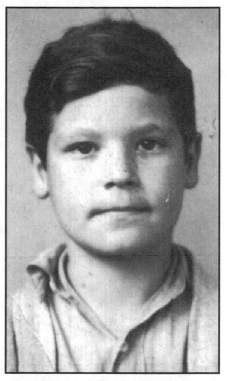

Gibeon J. Sullivan was born Dec. 29, 1831 and served in the War Between the States being inducted in St. Stephens, AL in December 1861. He died Nov. 1, 1914.

Enoch Sullivan at ten-years-old and in the 4th grade at Leroy High School.

This was the home of Leo and Annie Bell Gartman in Sunflower, AL, where Margie Louise Brewster and Evangelist Hazel Chain came from Louisiana in 1946 to hold services. It was here that Margie first met Enoch.

Margie Louise Brewster is shown with her guitar at age 12. Inset is a picture of her made in 1945, when she was 13, and lived in Delhi, LA.

Evangelist Hazel Chain and Margie Brewster are shown in this 1946 picture.

Enoch, Jerry and the Rev. Arthur Sullivan are shown in this 1948 photo.

Arthur and Florence Sullivan, Enoch and Emmett's parents. Circa 1951.

Proud mother Margie with first son, Clyde Dewayne, in 1951.

That's Brother Arthur Sullivan in the middle with the Bible and mandolin. Others left to right are Aubrey Sullivan, Hilton Taylor, Enoch Sullivan, Erlene Hudson Sullivan, Susie Sullivan Bryan, Margie Brewster Sullivan. Circa 1950.

COME SEE AND HEAR
SULLIVAN FAMILY

HEARD Each
Sun. 8:05 A.M.
To 8:30 AM.
Over
Radio Sta.
WJDB
630 on Dial
Thomasville Ala.

HEARD Each
Sat., 8:30 A.M.
To 8:45 A.M.
over
Radio Sta.
WPBB
1290 on Dial
Jackson, Ala.

Old Time
Gospel
Singing

With
String
Band

PLACE
DATE   TIME
ADMISSION
SPONSORED BY

Early Sullivan Family promotion poster, circa 1950. Seated are Enoch and Emmett; standing are Brother Arthur, Margie and Aubrey.

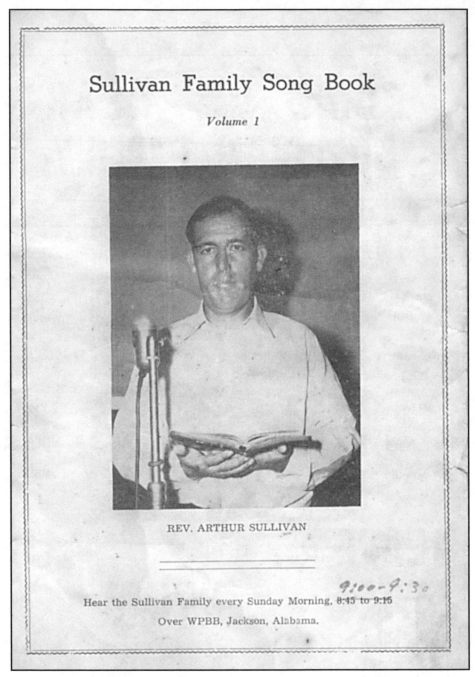

Sullivan Family Song Book

Volume 1

REV. ARTHUR SULLIVAN

Hear the Sullivan Family every Sunday Morning, 8:45 to 9:15

Over WPBB, Jackson, Alabama.

The first Sullivan Family Song Book, Volume 1, was issued in 1951. It measured 5 1/2 by 8 1/2 and contained eight pages. It featured a picture of Brother Arthur Sullivan Holding open his Bible on the front cover.

The Sullivans in 1952, Enoch, Emmett, Arthur and Aubrey.

Enoch is shown with their first child Clyde Dewayne in this 1952 photo.

The Sullivans are dressed for church in this 1958 photo. Standing are Emmett, Enoch and Margie. The children are Hugh Mac, Sharon and Debe, and they belong to Enoch and Margie.

Emmett, Enoch and Margie are shown in this 1958 picture, which was used on their show posters.

Patsy Cline is shown with Emmett and Enoch backstage at the Grand Ole Opry on November, 1962. Enoch always said he wish he had a copy of the picture. This book brought forth that wish.

Enoch and Margie are shown with Marvin Mathis, owner of station WSJC, 50,000 watts coming from Magee, MS. Photo taken in 1963.

The Sullivan Family performed for baseball legend Dizzy Dean at the opening of his museum in Wiggins, MS in 1966. Left to right are Enoch, Margie, Dizzy, Jerry and Emmett.

The Sullivan Family campaigned for Lurleen Wallace for Governor of Alabama in the late 60s. Left to right are A.R. Byrd, Jimmy Swan (who The Sullivans campaigned for Governor of Mississippi), Pat Massengail, Gov. Wallace, Enoch, Jerry and Emmett.

Song book, circa 1966. Left to right: Emmett, Jerry, Margie and Enoch.

Carl Story, third from left, is shown with the Sullivans during a live recording in 1971 at Philadelphia, MS. Enoch is shown on fiddle, Ronnie Dickerson is playing the bass and Margie is partially shown at right.

In 1971 The Sullivan Family signed a booking agreement with Bill Monroe's Bluegrass Booking Agency in Nashville, TN. Enoch is shown signing the contract. Left to right are Joe Stuart, Emmett Sullivan, Bill Monroe, Margie Sullivan, Chuck Campbell (who ran the agency) and Jerry Sullivan.

The Sullivan Family of 1971 are shown in this photo. That's young Marty Stuart with the mandolin. Left to right are Carl Jackson, Enoch, Margie, Ronnie Dickerson with the bass and Emmett.

Emmett, Howard Maples, Enoch, James Phillips and Margie made up the Sullivans in 1973. At the time they were broadcasting over WSCJ in Jackson, MS for J. L. Jones Furniture. The store also sponsored the Sullivans on WLBT-TV and WAPT-TV, both in Jackson.

The Sullivans in 1973 consisted of Enoch, Margie, Joe Stuart and Emmett.

The Sullivan Family Songbook cover of 1974. Left to right are Emmett, Jerry, Enoch and Margie.

The 1976 edition of ths Sullivan Family, left to right, Bob Burnham, Emmett, Enoch, Margie and James Phillips pictured going to the Grand Ole Opry.

In 1979, members of the Sullivan Family, left to right, were: Joe Stuart, Margie Sullivan, Emmett Sullivan, Lesa Sullivan, Enoch Sullivan, Vicky Cook, Paul MaHarrey and "Little Joe" Cook.

The 1980 edition of The Sullivans are, left to right, Lesa Sullivan, Emmett Sullivan, Vicky Cook, "Little Joe" Cook, Margie and Enoch.

The Sullivan Family of 1982 are, left to right, Richard Tew, Lesa Sullivan Bailey, Steve Carpenter, Margie, Emmett and Enoch.

Margie and Enoch Sullivan are shown with their band in this 1882 photo. Standing, left to right, are Steve Carpenter, Dikki Tew, Michael Bailey and Joy Deville.

This was the last Sullivan Family portrait taken in 1988 before the death of Enoch and Margie's son, Clyde Dewayne, Seated are Margie, Enoch and Debe Warren. Standing are Sharon Tew, Clyde Dewayne Sullivan, Hugh McArthur Sullivan and Lesa Bailey.

Grand Ole Opry star Charlie Louvin, third from left, has been a longtime friend of Margie and Enoch. At left is the Rev. A.L. Lyle of Louisiana. This 1990 photo was taken at the Bobby Smith Studio in Mobile, Al.

Margie and Enoch are shown in this 1968 photo taken at their home.

Sister Margie coming to you on television in Holland. Circa 1981.

Florence Loudine Bailey Sullivan, mother of Enoch and Emmett, is shown in this 1980 photo.

The late Bill Monroe, the originator of bluegrass music, was a very special and personal friend of Enoch and Margie Sullivan. This picture with the Grand Ole Opry star was taken in 1989 at Bean Blossom, Ind.

Bill Monroe and Enoch and Margie Sullivan are shown sitting on the front porch of "Uncle Pen's Cabin" at Bill's Park in Bean Blossom, IN in 1993. Holding the microphone is Rich Tew, Enoch and Margie's grandson.

Margie and Enoch are shown with twice Louisiana Governor Jimmie Davis in this 1995 photo. Davis, who will turn 100 on Sept. 10, 1999, is a member of the Country Music Hall of Fame.

Alabama Governor Fob James is pictured with Margie and Enoch in this 1998 photo.

Enoch Sullivan and his fiddle, photo made in 1993.

Enoch and Margie are shown with Jim and Jesse, the Virginia Boys, and long time stars of the Grand Ole Opry. Picture was taken at Canton, TX, June 1998.

Sonny, left and Bobby, right, the world-famous Osborne brothers from the world-famous Grand Ole Opry, are shown with Enoch and Margie at the Canton, TX Bluegrass Festival in June 1998.

Enoch and Margie, along with Joy Deville on bass are shown performing at Canton, TX in June 1998.

Legendary bluegrass singer Mac Wiseman, center, visits with Enoch and Margie at the June 1998 Blugrass Festival in Canton, TX.

Sister Margie puts her heart and soul into a song at the 1998 Festival at Canton, TX., while Joy Deville backs her on bass and Enoch on guitar.

Dr. Ralph Stanley, leader of The Clinch Mountain Boys from McClure, VA, visits with Enoch and Margie at the Canton, TX festival in June 1998.

The late Emmett Sullivan and his wife, Louise, 1992.

The Emmett Sullivan Family today is shown above. Seated is his widow, Louise. Standing left to right are Mechelle (Shelly) Parnell, David and Zina Motes. In the inset picture is their oldest daughter, Renee', who was killed in an auto accident Sept. 9, 1989. This photo was taken two weeks before her death. She was their oldest daughter.

Children of the late **Dewayne Sullivan** and his wife **Pauline Johnson Sullivan**

General G. (Gibb) Sullivan

Haley Ruth Sullivan

Clyde Dewayne Sullivan II and his wife Cathy

Lesa Sullivan Bailey and her husband Allen are shown in this photo. At left is their daughter Jessica. Standing are their twins, Jennie and Jake.

Barry and Heather Sullivan Walker shown above. They are Enoch and Margie's oldest granddaughter and the mother of great granddaughter Kathlyn.

Enoch and Margie's only great grandchild is Kathlyn M. Walker, born July 2, 1996.

Hugh McArthur Sullivan, Enoch and Margie's son, is shown with his wife, Nelda Grace. Their oldest daughter is Heather Sullivan Walker, top right. Their twin sons are Hugh and Heath and their other daughter is Heidi, at right next to her mother.

This is Debbie, the middle daughter of Enoch and Margie and their fourth child, she was born in 1957. She is shown with her husband, Mark Warren, and standing are their sons, Waylon and Brandon.

This is Sharon, the oldest daughter and third child of Enoch and Margie, born in 1956. At left is their son Richard and at right is her husband Richard (Dikki) Tew.

Chapter 10

Going to Holland and Other Countries
Overseas Trips Develop During 1980's

MARGIE: There's always been the force behind the Sullivan Family much greater than we can control and much greater than we can explain. I know it's because of the calling of the Lord in our lives that we've been able to do what we've done. It's been caused first of all by the blessings from the Lord and then because of our many good friends over the world.

We were fortunate to take three trips to Holland. The first was Nov. 1-15, 1980. The second was Nov. 1-22, 1981 and the last was Aug. 6-21, 1983.

It started in the 1970's when we met a group of Dutchmen from Holland. We met them at a bluegrass festival in Lavonia, GA and they were impressed with our music and style. They listened to the show and then came around and made themselves known. Luke Lahmers was the head spokesman. He spoke English well and it was real easy to understand him. We all became instant friends. I remember that each of the seven bought a full set of the Sullivan Family materials. They carried them back to their home country, enjoyed them and corresponded with us. I well remember how Luke said they would very much like to see the Sullivan Family come to the Netherlands. We thought about the possibility, but it seemed to be impossible to us. Enoch and I both at a period of time began to think about the Dutchmen. He said, "I wish you would contact them; we haven't heard from them in while. It just might be possible that we could visit their country and present our music over there."

ENOCH: We had actually met the group five or six years prior to the time we went to Holland. They were in America searching the history of country music and had gone to the Grand Ole Opry.

MARGIE: I had moved our office into a mobile home in our yard and somehow in the move lost their address and phone number. So I really didn't know how to contact them. When I moved my desk a card fell out. It was amazing to us. We were just talking about the people in Holland and then we found the card with the phone number and address.

I laid the card on top of the desk and said, "There's only one thing that I can do now and that's contact them and tomorrow when I get all my chores finished I will do that."

In the meantime, that day, in the mail we had an airmail letter from Luke. He said, "Where are the Sullivans?" That's how he opened his letter. He had his phone number on the letter and I called him the next day. We set November 1980 as a time for us to go to Holland, Belgium and some other countries. This was our first trip overseas and we were very excited about it. I didn't know how to arrange it, since it was our first. On the other hand, Luke knew how to set the dates and did so for a three-week period.

ENOCH: When Luke called, it just seemed like a lot of things happened. It was the right time and nobody seemed to have to put too much effort into it. It just seemed to be. It was that way with arranging the trip. We had to get passports and birth certificates. Right down toward the last we went to Nashville and saw Joel and Labreeska Hemphill. They were good friends and she took us on a shopping spree and bought me a hat. She wanted me to have a hat to go to Holland. She's crazy and full of fun and a wonderful lady. We had a lot of fun shopping for the trip, but there were an awful lot of business arrangements that had to be made.

MARGIE: Yes, we worked to buy clothes and get ready for the trip. There was one thing holding us back - and that was money. When we checked, we found it would cost $7,500 to get six people to Holland. We knew we couldn't just go with the tickets alone, that we had to have some money to carry us through a three week stay.

We prayed about it as we had no funds to speak of and surely not enough to do that. We had at different times mortgaged our home to do different things, but Enoch and I made a pact that we would never do that again. We always wanted a roof over the heads of our children that couldn't be taken away. It got close to the time we had to purchase the tickets and it looked like we would have to cancel the tour. I was really distressed because I felt we should go. I believed there was a need for us and that we could minister to people if we went. I really prayed about it and told Enoch, "Honey, we will just have to pray about it and if it's the Lord's will, it will be worked out so we can go."

In praying, it was as if the Lord spoke, not in an audible voice, but he let me understand something. And it was that every time we wanted something ourselves, we would go and mortgage the house to get the money. It was like the Lord condemned me for not being willing to mortgage the house for the tickets for something He needed us to do. I was even afraid to approach Enoch with the subject, because I was afraid he wouldn't go along with it. I waited around two or three days and it got to three days before the deadline for purchasing the tickets.

Finally, one day he came in and it seemed he was

in a good mellow mood and I said, "Honey, I know how we can go to Holland." He asked, "How?" I replied, "Well, we could mortgage the house." Enoch looked at me and said, "Well, if it means that much to you to go, then do it."

So I went to the bank and mortgaged the house to finance the trip. That was the most unforgettable journey of all we've ever made.

ENOCH: It all fell into place. I approached Lance Leroy of Nashville about going with us. He was highly versed in music and said he'd be glad to go. He formerly managed Lester Flatt and Earl Scruggs and the Foggy Mountain Boys. After they dissolved the act, Lance continued to manager Lester until he died. The band going with us was Emmett, Little Joe Cook, his sister Vicki and our daughter Lesa. We had a fine band.

MARGIE: There was a certain amount of excitement about getting to be able to present our music to people in another country. What was so awesome was the anointing of the spirit of the Lord upon the songs we sang. We had an interpreter do the introductions for the songs and there were some places where you were not allowed to testify. That really distressed me until the Lord opened my understanding. What I learned was that when you couldn't say it, you sang it in a song. That's when I realized those interpreters were telling the meaning of the songs we were singing.

I realized that every song was a sermon within itself. Say for instance, *Walking My Lord Up Calvary Hill*. That song is the complete story of Our Lord's death, burial and resurrection and the reason He died. Then, of course, we sang *I Know That I've Been Born Again*. You couldn't help but realize there was a deep experience that you could have with the Lord; that you could actually be born again of water and of the spirit of God. When we were singing *He Will Calm The Troubled Waters Of Your Soul*, it was like He was saying, "I have a remedy for your troubles and your problems. I'll take them on my shoulders and bear them." He said, "Bring your problems, bring your troubles, bring your cares to me because I care for you." That was the message we carried to Europe. I don't know how many people were blessed from it, but I know one person who was richly blessed and that is me because I obeyed what the Lord wanted me to do.

On one occasion we went to a town in Belgium to a "Florala Festival." It was a combination of many groups from many countries, in fact 20 different countries. There was a group of actors and actresses from England who did a Shakespeare play. They had Polish dancers and from the United States they had us do bluegrass gospel, which was really a thrill and honor for us.

ENOCH: They had an Irish band and we played with them for the finale. They had the sound a lot like us and Bill Monroe - with mandolins, fiddles, guitars and an Irish harp.

MARGIE: We later learned this festival was put on by the Catholic churches of Belgium. We got there a little late and all but two rooms had been taken at the motel. There were six of us and we needed three rooms. The promoter came and said two of us could stay in a private home. Enoch and I said we would stay in the home so the band could have the motel rooms.

When we got to the home to freshened-up for our appearance, we met a middle-aged gentleman with graying hair. He was very congenial and very knowledgeable of the English language and he was easy to talk to. I could tell right away he was a man of importance and that he was a man of great and vast

117

knowledge. I had not been told he was a priest. His name was escapes me, but he was pastor of a Catholic church in Belgium.

He showed us to the third floor bedroom for us to rest awhile. I'm one of those people who is full of energy and it is hard to stop me, so I couldn't rest. I went downstairs in search of the lady of the house. I thought maybe we could visit or she could show me around. I was in a new country and wanted to see everything. I'm curious - I wanted to see it all.

On the first floor the gentleman was alone in his office. He invited me to come in and as I sat down I thought the lady of the house would bring us some tea or something. I was looking forward to meeting her and having some time with a lady. No one ever came. He asked if I would like some tea and I said that I would drink cola, if he had one. He got us both something to drink. I looked around his office and I was trying to guess in what profession he was engaged.

I saw so many books. The walls were lined with them and with some of the most beautiful paintings I ever saw. I'm just blunt, I guess, maybe too straightforward sometimes, but I don't mean any harm by it. I am just curious; I wanted to know, so I asked, "You must be a writer?"

He looked at all the books and he knew where I was coming from and he replied, "No." We talked a little further and I said, "Maybe you're a painter, because I see all these beautiful paintings."

He said, "No ma'am, I'm a Catholic priest." I now realized why there was no lady around and I was definitely glad I didn't ask about his wife.

Our conversation turned toward our work and what we were doing in Belgium, Holland and Europe.

118

I told him that for many years we had been singing bluegrass gospel and that we had done it as a ministry. I said it was more to us than just entertainment. We were trying to reach hearts, to bless and encourage them and to help them find the Lord if they didn't know Him. I looked at him and said, "You know, what made the difference in my life is that when I was nine years old, I had a born again experience." He raised both hands and said, "So have I! I have been born again. I'm what you call a charismatic Catholic priest. I have had that experience as well."

I knew then that the Lord had led us to his house, for us to have the opportunity to talk and encourage each other and appreciate each other. I really do appreciate people wherever I find them in whatever walk of life and whatever they call themselves. To be a child of God first is most important. I think you know when you are and I think that most everybody knows when they're not.

The next day we were privileged to be in the same priest's church. It was very big, one of the largest churches I've ever seen. It was packed to capacity. I wondered how our music would be received. They made a list of the songs we were going to do and the interpreter told the congregation what each of them meant. We did seven songs that morning and were richly blessed.

ENOCH: I've never felt a church service like that. I never felt the presence of the Lord the way I felt it there. I don't believe I ever felt that way or was received in any church like that.

MARGIE: It seemed there was such a presence of the Lord there. You could tell the Lord was ministering through the songs and it was really awesome. At the close of service, the priest asked me to come up and he presented me with flowers, which is

119

very common in those countries. They give you flowers. Almost every home you go in, they give you a fresh bouquet. It's one of the common courtesies. By the same token, when you go into a home, you should always take the flowers to your host.

The priest asked me if I wanted to make any comments about our tour. I replied that it had been the greatest pleasure in the world to visit Europe and their beautiful country of Belgium and to have the opportunity to play the festival. I said, "We were chosen to represent the United States with our music, which is the highest honor you could pay us. It's an honor to come from America and represent what we do - our style, our kind and our form of music. I really do hope we have represented our country well, but what I hope more so is that we have represented our Lord in the fashion He should be represented." When I said that, the audience began to applaud. The priest came up and kissed me on one cheek and then on the other. I didn't know what it meant until we were back in the car. One of the Dutchmen said, "Do you know what the priest just did?"

I replied, "Well, I guess I don't exactly know the meaning." He said, "That was when he blessed you."

I thought that was one of the nicest things that could have ever been done. It was like he understood our message, our reason and our contact with the people and with the Lord. It really moved me. What was so strange about it was when we got back to Holland; the news had already reached there. I don't know how, but they already knew about how the priest had blessed me.

ENOCH: We were gone for 21 days and you can't believe the reception we received in Holland. There is no way to put it in words. I remember on opening night, we went by Germany and played to a standing ovation. It seemed everybody who was interested in country music in Germany, Switzerland, Sweden and Belgium had come to see us.

The next day after we played the church in Belgium, we played a big rose garden in Holland. When we got there, they couldn't handle all the people. They had five stages set up. We used one and there were other bands on the other stages. We sang our first song and the people came over and just swarmed us. They had to get the security guards to hold them back. They came around pushing and shoving as we were coming down the steps. They wanted autographs. They didn't mean to do it, but they were pushing so hard they over balanced Margie and she fell into the bass fiddle and cut her head. We were just pressed in with people. Then they took us to the back and got us into another place to rest for the next show. The promoter came in and asked, "Would you have any problem closing the show? We had you set to go back and a country band to close, but with your publicity and being such a hit with the people, would you have a problem with waiting until last and closing?" We closed the show. They finally had to come and get us off stage. To this day, I can't believe it.

On that first trip, we did television shows. We had to go to the communist television station to record them. That was quite an experience. They did things differently there. You recorded a thirty-minute show, they paid you a flat rate for doing it and they owned the show. That was the only legal way to do it.

We played so many important programs and we did work for Tross Radio. The reception was different from anything we received in the U.S. or anywhere else in the world.

The first night in Holland, we opened with *Traveling the Highway Home*, a quick driving tune. We

121

had a great band. Emmett was on banjo, Vicki was on the guitar but switched with the banjo, Little Joe worked the mandolin and also did twin fiddles. Margie was on guitar and Lesa played bass. It all moved so fast. The very first night we worked in a big cathedral and they didn't have the proper sound equipment. Lance took the one microphone, knelt on one knee in front and held it while we were singing.

When Margie sang *Matthew Twenty-Four* the crowd called her back to sing it again. We were just scheduled to do a couple of numbers because it was a big show. On the second show, the crowd would not sit down. They were stomping the floor and hollering in unison, "We want more." The third show was the same way. I tried to talk to the promoter and tell him to go ahead with the show. He told me, "No, you come back. We can't handle them. They want to hear you." We had to go on and on. They just would not stop. We finished out the complete show. When they finally let us go, they just dismissed the crowd. The show was over. The folks lined up and bought every single recorded piece of material we had brought with us. We carried as much as they would allow us on the plane. All the Sullivan Family recordings sold for $25 each. That night we had to send back home and have more shipped to us.

They had booked us into the third floor of a hotel. Lance, Emmett and Little Joe were all in the same room. In the middle of the night Emmett had to use the bathroom which was down a flight of stairs. We heard the most awful noise in the wee hours. Emmett had started down those little short steps and his foot slipped. He skidded down the stairway on his bottom and I think it burned the hide all the way down to his knees.

Little Joe was just a young lad and Emmett "pranked" with him a lot. The next morning I heard an awful commotion. Emmett was trying to get Little Joe to examine where he had been hurt. Little Joe was saying, "No, there'll never be any days like that!" It was all a lot of fun.

MARGIE: I remember the girls had a room to themselves. It was so cold the icicles were hanging 15 inches from the hotel roof. We had been out on a show and our clothes were not sufficient for that weather. The girls were cold. They turned the stove on and forgot to turn it off. In the night the fire alarms went off. We didn't know what was happening, but the rooms were filled with smoke. One of the girls had already been overcome with smoke and the other one was wild eyed.

ENOCH: You talk about fear, when that fire alarm went off, that crew woke up, Buddy. Little Joe was running up and down the hallway in his underwear hollering, "Get my sister. Get my sister."

Not long after that the fire chief came and wanted to know what happened. I thought we'd had it, but when they saw there was no damage, everything was all right. It was just another bill to pay.

MARGIE: We stayed in the home of Mr. and Mrs. Luke Lamers. They were so cordial and make us feel at home. Their courtesies were above and beyond. They even cooked special food they found in a cookbook for folks from the United States. We enjoyed their family, especially their three teenage daughters.

We also met Dr. Von Botman at Wogrium, N. Holland. He treated Enoch when he got sick with flu. He and his wife were very good to us. There were so many good folks we met over there and in later years some of them came to visit us in the states.

ENOCH: While there we got a chance to record

an album *Live In Holland*. They set up the recording session at a place called "Fiddler's Farm." It was a big showcase place for their country music. Every time we played it was to a standing ovation, again and again.

Lance Leroy is a man who is a great authority on bluegrass music. He, Emmett and I were talking about the business. He said something that I am real proud of. Lance said, "This beats all I've ever seen. This music needs to be brought over here. Boys, I've traveled a lot of places and this is the greatest reception I ever saw for the music. I traveled with Lester and Earl at the height of the power of their band. The Sullivan Family right now is undoubtedly the most powerful band I ever heard play bluegrass. You've got the most powerful approach and the hardest drive. You have the same thing going for you right now that Lester and Earl had at their zenith. I didn't think I'd ever hear anybody but them do it, but I hear it again now in what you're doing."

Back to the recording, Luke Lamers, our Dutch guide, promoter, friend and booking agent, introduced it on one side and Lance Leroy introduced the other side. It's a big part of the history of bluegrass gospel music as the Sullivan Family does it.

From that very recording, we got opportunities where we could have toured in Australia and Japan. We did a cruise. I was asked if I would do an interview with a Russian reporter. He wanted to talk about our style of music. I said I'd be glad to talk to anybody about that. I remember while we were talking on the ship that he drew a sketch of me. I still have it.

One of the most interesting people we met on the tour was a man named Norris. He was a colored man, a county singer, who was born in Florida. His dad was a minister and they had moved to Holland and he never came back to the states. He married and raised his family there. The only difference in him and Charlie Pride is that he did imitations. Charlie Pride sings a lot like Hank Williams did, always good country music. Norris could sing like Hank Snow, Jimmie Rodgers and he could yodel. We met a lot of great musicians in that country.

The next year, 1980, Lance booked some other bluegrass acts into Europe. It had opened up a great market for bluegrass and some added country music as well. There was a group that came called "Ground Speed" and they did progressive bluegrass from Holland to the U.S. They were great. Boxcar Willie was already famous in Europe and George Hamilton IV was there at the same time we were.

We went again in 1981 for the Evangelistic Organization. There were so many places they wanted us to go. Margie's sister, Nadine Brewster, went with us. Our band was about the same except for Emmett. He didn't want to fly, so he stayed home. Our son-in-law Dicki Tew was with us on guitar in addition to Little Joe. We had Lesa on bass and Mike Bailey on banjo. They released a song for us that I wrote called *Gospel Train*. It was an instant hit and went to number four in all categories of music in *The Country Gazzette*. That's a country music publication in Europe.

The Evangelistic Organization released another album for us on Continental Sounds Records entitled, *The Sullivan Family Remembers The Louvin Brothers*. It sold great there, too.

MARGIE: Even though we worked so hard day and night for the Evangelistic Organization, we had left a little time for sight-seeing. I think we had one day off. We went to see the windmills and they showed us how the oldest ones worked with wooden gears. We saw the old wooden ships, dating way back that they had in storage.

Thanks to my friend, Mrs. Von Botman, I got to see the most famous painting in the word, *Night Watch*. We went by trolley car to Amsterdam to the Reiks Museum. You can also tour the city by boat. We went to see a lot of the places including the home of Corrie Ten Boom.

The three tours to Holland did a lot for the Sullivan Family's career. It really broadened our work, our publicity and promotion, as well as our outlook. It was amazing to me that our music carried us that far.

The more I saw the Dutch people, the more I saw their influences on our people back in the states. We've adopted so many of their customs.

ENOCH: Take the state of Wisconsin, it's almost like Holland, down to the dairy cattle. We toured the dairies. It's a great country for cheese, like Wisconsin. They told me the foundation stock for their dairy herds was from Wisconsin.

MARGIE: We crossed the Rhine River where Gen. George Patton crossed and our boys fought. We went to the American Cemetery where our soldier boys are buried and honored so highly by the Dutch people. They gave them 45-55 acres of their valuable land for a cemetery.

ENOCH: I had a cousin, James Victor Sullivan, killed there. They sent his remains back to Alabama for burial at St. Stephens.

I'll be forever grateful to the Dutch people for making my song *Gospel Train* a number one song. I always wonder why things happen. I still have the *Country Gazzette* magazine where it's listed in four categories of music. Two notches down, Bill Monroe is listed. I told them at the time, "Don't you ever tell Mr. Bill that we're ahead of him. He might fire us all."

I couldn't understand why a song that we would do would go to number four. I thought, "Well, it's a train song, so I guess we might as well just give credit to Boxcar Willie, because he went over there and did all those train songs. He had country music wide open for us." I didn't even realize when we released the song that we had such a powerful hit over there.

On a sight seeing tour, they took us to the little church where the pilgrims left when they decided to settle in America. It impressed me greatly that our founding fathers started out in a little church in Rotterdam that measured about 30 feet by 40 feet and seated no more than 50 people. I walked down the steps where the pilgrims walked and got into the boat. Its name was "Speedwell." They sailed around to England where they got financed and got on the Mayflower to come to America.

It shows that if you have a dream, no matter how big or small, if you'll stay with it, that dream just might come to pass and sometimes far exceed your greatest expectations.

Chapter 11

The Louvin Brothers Music Park

It came to Enoch Sullivan one night as a dream. Or was it a vision? It concerned the old homeplace of Charlie and Ira Louvin, two of the great names in the field of country music.

The Louvins were actually born Loudermilks near Henagar in Section, AL. Ira the oldest, was born April 21, 1924, and brother, Charlie, came along July 7, 1927.

The two had a harmony that only brothers can have. They had just started in show business when World War II broke out and both entered the Army. After the war, their first big break came when they signed with WNOX in Knoxville, TN to appear on the "Mid-Day Merry-Go Round." Charlie was recalled to the army at the outbreak of the Korean War in the early 1950's. When the brothers reunited they joined Capitol Records and later the Grand Ole Opry in 1955 and had a very successful career.

Because of the inability to get along, the brothers parted ways in 1963 and Ira was killed in an auto accident in Williamsburg, MO on Father's Day 1965. Charlie continued as a solo artist and enjoyed a very successful career.

Charlie bought the old homeplace in Henagar many years ago to help his ailing father who was becoming worse each day from his health problems.

It was in 1982 that Charlie had a conversation with a man that would make drastic changes in his life. Enoch Sullivan told Charlie he had dreams and visions concerning the old Louvin Brothers home place. He told Charlie, who was living in Nashville, TN that it would be the place to build a music park.

Enoch asked if he could look at the old home place and when Charlie agreed, he drove down from Nashville to meet Enoch who was driving up from Chatom to Henagar. That was in March 1982.

They walked through the woods on the property and crawled when the brush and briars were too dense to get the scope of the land. Enoch told Charlie that the land he saw in reality was the same land he had seen in his dreams. The lay of the land and the gradual sloping to the elevated stage, the natural terracing and ease of visibility after clearing were just as his dream foretold.

Enoch's dream was what gave Charlie the inspiration to begin construction. In June 1982 he began clearing land and laying foundations for one of the most beautiful music parks anywhere.

Charlie named the festival, "May On The Mountain" and the first one was held May 6-7-8, 1983. In addition to the Sullivan Family, Charlie had Roy Acuff, Grandpa Jones and many other country and bluegrass acts there for his opening.

In addition to the music park, Charlie had the Louvin Brothers Museum on the grounds. Charlie had started the museum in 1981 in Hendersonville, TN., near Nashville.

Louvin operated the music park until 1992 when he moved himself and wife, Betty, and the museum to Bell Buckle, TN. Louvin said he shut the park down because he had to commute to Nashville to work and also the Alabama entertainment taxes are so very high. The festival just wasn't economically worth all the effort and upkeep.

Charlie and Betty will celebrate their 50th Wedding Anniversary on September 18, 1999.

Chapter 12

Mountaintop and Valleys
The Decade of the 1980's

ENOCH: Of course, the highlight of the 1980's was our three trips to Holland and other European countries. It seems that this period was some of the richest years for our work.

We went back to Canada with Charlie Louvin and the Rev. Freddie Clark and his family from Houlton, ME. The kids were little and they couldn't play music. But they were little troopers and we enjoyed those years. So many doors still open from those times.

MARGIE: There are mountain tops and there are valleys and you have to deal with grief along with the good times. In January 1988 we lost Granny, Enoch's mother. Then in December the same year, I lost my precious mother. In August 1989 we lost our oldest son, Wayne, and that was the hardest blow we've ever been hit with. Just 20 days after Wayne's death, Emmett lost his oldest daughter, Rene, who was 30 years old. She was killed in a head-on car crash. In November, our bass fiddle player Joy Deville, lost her father, Harold Deville. You have to deal with the grief along with the good times.

The Sullivan Family are real people, too, with real problems and losses. I can say from the heart that through it all, the Lord is always there whether you're on top of the mountain or down in the valley. He's there to hold your hand and help you. We got through those years of sorrow with the help of the good Lord and a lot of good friends.

ENOCH: One of the things I've been concerned

about during this span of time is that in view of all the work Lance Leroy, the Sullivan Family and Luke Lamers did and all the other people in Holland, we failed to get the recognition for our music. I'm not speaking selfishly for myself, but the Sullivan Family band was there. We failed to get recognition from the country music and southern gospel music associations or business. The Bluegrass Music Association was very small back then and there wasn't a lot we could do. But, I still think it should have been publicized a lot more.

It was a great stepping stone for southern gospel, for bluegrass gospel and for country music, both progressive and traditional. Since that time, Ricky Scaggs has been to Holland, to all the places we first played there.

There are other older bands that need to be credited, the Bailes Brothers and Charlie Louvin for examples. While we were on our first tour in Europe, we met Mr. Wade Mainer. He and his wife, and the Mainer's Mountaineers were founding fathers of the old time string band country and bluegrass music along with Bill Monroe. I think there should have been a lot more promotion and publicity on that.

We were still going strong throughout the '80's with our music. I would like to make another trip to Holland, in a high fashion that the music deserves. They've approached us many times about going to Japan. I'd love to make a trip to Japan and I'd like to go to Australia. I've always wanted to do some work in Ireland. I think there are a lot of Sullivans over there.

During the '80's we did some work in Missouri and met Chuck Stearman. He had a bluegrass music association going good in Missouri and Arkansas. He was a great fan of the Louvin Brothers. He assisted us with the promotion of "May On The Mountain" when

Charlie opened the festival at the Louvin Brothers' home place.

Chuck said, "I'll help you with the promotion out here if you'll help me bring in a show at Nashville. We want to give some awards to some deserving people up there and have a big show in the wintertime. Would you go and help me with that?"

I know Hal Durham, who was manager of the Grand Ole Opry, real well. He is one of the most honorable men I ever met. Little Joe and I met Chuck Stearman and Joe Stuart there. We met with the Nashville Chamber of Commerce and Chuck told them what he wanted to do. They pledged their support. They made the arrangements and we got the deal through. We ask Mr. Durham for his help and he was all for it. He said he wished he could help us more with playing our music, but at that time the Opry and WSM radio were separated and he didn't have anything to do with the programming. What we did proved to be one of the greatest shows and I am glad we were able to be part of bringing it to town.

At one time, we were able to bring Charlie Louvin and Jimmy Martin and his Sunny Mountain Boys on the Spigma show at the Sheraton Inn in Nashville, TN. We had just recorded the album *The Sullivan Family Remembers The Louvin Brothers*. We concluded the show with *Will The Circle Be Unbroken*. Jimmy sang it and you can't believe the reception-five standing ovations. The show is still going on and I'm proud of it and what Chuck is doing. I just want him to work the Sullivan Family more, if he will.

MARGIE: We did our first Bluegrass Gospel Convention in Nashville during the '80's. We worked a second one at Opryland and got good response from both of them.

ENOCH: I remember that our late friend filmed the first one, Buddy Banes from television station Channel 9 in Tupelo, MS. His wife Kay is still active with the program and I'd like to get over there and see if we can get some of those videos.

Chuck Campbell booked us at those conventions. He was booking for Mr. Bill Monroe at the time. Mr. Bill mentioned it to all the bluegrass bands at fanfare and they all came over and helped us.

That included Jim and Jesse, The Osborne Brothers, Mac Wiseman, Bill Monroe and his Bluegrass Boys, James Monroe, Bill Harrell and his band and Carl Story and the Rambling Mountaineers. We really appreciated all of them doing that.

MARGIE: We were called to do a homecoming with our good friends and neighbors, The Bibletones from Gulfport, MS. That was during the '80's and they are a very popular southern gospel group. We were thrilled and honored to be a part of their homecoming.

Chapter 13

The Death of Emmett Sullivan

MARGIE: Emmett Sullivan hung in there with us all the time and was right there with that old banjo. People just loved him and he loved people. He was a big third part with his singing and playing.

His family backed him. His little wife, Louise, didn't like traveling much, in fact she was carsick every time she went anywhere. We really wanted her to go with us because it would have been easier for Emmett to take her along, but she couldn't travel. She told Emmett she would stay home, take care of the family and work, thus enabling him to go. She loved his playing and not only stood by him, but stood by us. She was appreciated because like Brother Hudson said at Emmett's funeral, "She could have been selfish and said 'No' you have to stay and help me raise the children and make the living here at home. But instead, she was willing to loan him to the public and to the work so that they could hear his good banjo playing."

He had a style all his own, and to me it's never been equaled and it can't be duplicated. I never stand on the stage that I don't almost hear those notes that he would hit if he were playing behind us.

Emmett was a prankster. He was the one who made everyone laugh. I don't guess there would have been many laughs a lot of times if it hadn't been for him. He 'pranked' with me, with Enoch, the public (especially the kids), and everybody that ever came and joined the Sullivan Family. He was a good practical joker. But he had a serious, loving side, too, and he was kind. I'll have to say that he always showed me the greatest respect. He was my brother-in-law and that meant so much to me.

They say that in two weeks time, staying with somebody on the road, you can learn more about them than you do in a lifetime trying to get acquainted with them. He knew all my good points and all my bad ones and he loved me in spite of them and was always so considerate of me. He was a jewel. To Enoch and me, he was like our oldest son. He was only 13 when Enoch and I married and I used to laugh and say, "Well son, I almost half raised you." He had a great and wonderful relationship, Emmett, Enoch and I.

Lou, as I lovingly call Honey, has been a great support to us and we'll always love her. She'll always be a part of the Sullivan Family. Her fine children, David, Rene, Zina and Shelly, have earned our love and gratitude for their help in keeping the Sullivan Family going.

ENOCH: Emmett's death on April 10, 1993, was the greatest loss we ever suffered in our music. In the last months of his life, he couldn't make long trips due to his declining health. I wanted him to go, but I didn't want him to risk his health. He did some local work with different ones and us. He worked with Don Wiley of Jonesville, LA at some of the festivals. He was able to do that when we were gone on long trips.

His heart was in it and he always encouraged us. When something like this happens, you go on, but you feel the loss and it hurts terribly and you can't express it to a lot of people. I miss him. He was there when I left and he was there when I got back. Even though he couldn't do those long rides, I could count on him to watch over things until I got home. I knew everything would be as good as if I was there, or better. He knew how to manage the farm and he was a master mechanic. He and his son, David, and Billy Prebble kept the farm and the vehicles all going.

Along the end he was so very sick. He was inducted into the Alabama Country Music Hall of Fame and we saw where the Sullivan Family was going to be inducted into Bill Monroe's Bluegrass Hall of Fame. But Emmett didn't live long enough to see it. The inductions were not until the fall and he died April 10, 1993.

He died from an aneurysm of the brain. His death was instantaneous. He was drinking coffee with his wife, Louise, and his next door neighbors, Mr. and Mrs. Gary Padgett. He started to stand and fell forward and onto the floor. Gary administered CPR and an ambulance was called. But he was pronounced "dead on arrival."

Friends from many states attended his funeral including 25 ministers. The last instrumental played was *My Last Days on Earth* by Bill Monroe as friends and family filed past the casket. He now rests in Clear Water Cemetery near Wagarville, AL with his ancestors who went on before him. We miss his humor and his music but we carry on in the way he would wish us to do until we join him and the band will once again be complete.

So, it was a happy time, yet a sad time because Emmett was not there with us at the induction ceremonies. His wife was there and so many friends from far away came. Bill Monroe and his son, James, came to pay their respects.

I will always remember Emmett as a hard working man, a banjo picker that ranked with the best of them, a real trooper, and most of all as my beloved brother.

Chapter 14

Looking Back On Emmett

Edd Stifflemire lives in Grove Hill, AL, where he is town clerk, but on the side he is a part-time musician. He writes the following recollections of the Sullivan Family.

"The story of the Sullivan Family began before my time with the Rev. Arthur Sullivan, Enoch and Emmett's dad. He was a minister and founder of the singing group. Although I feel I knew him because of the stories I have heard, I really didn't and therefore won't try to discuss him.

"I have been acquainted with the Sullivans since around 1970. I cannot remember when or where I first met them, but my primary interest was in Emmett because he played banjo. I spent lots of time at his house 'harassing' him to help me play banjo. He did so with the patience of Job. I also frequented Sullivan Family shows and church dates and Emmett would ride with me when possible. I stayed in a state of hysteria, as Emmett was more full of life and fun than anyone else I've ever known. He could find humor in almost every situation and he believed in keeping laughter therapy going most of the time. I laughed until I hurt every time I was around him.

"As far as the show and the business were concerned, Emmett kept the music in the right gear and groove. When something wasn't going right he would drive the banjo into the microphone and force everyone else to follow his lead. That worked well most of the time, but occasionally someone would be filling in on bass or just visiting with the group that just would not get in the groove and drive the music up to par. In that case, Emmett would say that he carried

141

that person on his shoulder through the entire program. Emmett was also the lead transportation engineer (bus driver) and saw to details such as off loading and loading, the sound system, record display, etc.

"Enoch (or Jody as Emmett and others have called him), calls the shot from a business perspective. That is, he decides which dates are feasible, when to leave, what musicians to use, etc. Now that Emmett is gone, Enoch is the only 'transportation engineer' and he is the center of the music because he starts most of the tunes that they do. This came to pass because he, Miss Margie and Joy Deville organized things after Emmett was unable to travel so they could keep the core of the music solo and carry on with the other sidemen of varying capabilities. Enoch's fiddling is solid and bold and is always a crowd pleaser.

"Enoch loves cows. Charlie Louvin made that announcement at a church singing they worked together. Charlie said, and I know it to be correct, that Enoch would rather be with his cows (he has 130) doing something for, with, to or about them, than he had to eat. That's a lot said because he does love to eat. But to further drive home the point, anyone in the band can tell you that they commonly leave late for a show date because he can't leave the cows.

"Miss Margie is the spiritual center of the group. Her relationship with God, and the divine strength and leadership that God has provided through her, keeps the group going when it otherwise would fail. She'll gladly testify at every opportunity about her relationship with God, but it is not necessary. It is evident from looking at her life and just listening to the 'soul' in the songs she sings.

"Margie is also the vocal center of the group. She has a wonderful voice that is crisp, clear and full. It is

142

as sweet as heaven's chorus and as full and projecting as Moses on the mountain. Every song she sings keeps Molly O'Day and Martha Carson alive and sets the atmosphere, regardless of location, to that of a brush arbor or tent revival. Audiences at festivals, churches and numerous venues in between love her and her singing.

"The Sullivans drink coffee as strong as asphalt. My first experience was at Emmett's house. His wife, Louise would serve coffee and it was so strong it would melt the spoon. Emmett used a lot of sugar and cream so I started telling Louise to fix mine like Emmett's. I still couldn't drink it. Enoch and Margie make it the same way. When she serves me coffee, she dilutes it fifty percent with hot water and it is still too strong. They all say they discovered long ago that it took a lot less water to make coffee than most folks thought.

"The Sullivans love Cajun food. A few years ago, on the opening night of their festival, they had a 'pot luck' supper at their house. I was invited and enjoyed the visit but the pot held no luck for me. It was a Cajun concoction cooked in a wash pot (a big iron pot that sits on the ground and you build a fire around it) and contained everything but the dishrag. It had several sea critters, sausage, corn, rice, lots of seasoning, etc.

"To me it looked like something that had already been eaten, but everyone thought it was fine. I successfully refused any of the mixture for awhile, but at last one of the ladies would not let me refuse it any longer. I accepted a plate of the stuff and moved to the open front door of the house. By this time dark had arrived and the people had moved inside.

"I stood in the door and stirred in my plate while visiting with people sitting in the living room. I never took a bite but continued to play with it and try to figure my way out of the dilemma. At last the people all seemed occupied with each other and no one was focused on me. At the same time a cat meowed at the end of the house. I eased down the steps and through the darkness to the corner of the house. I called the cat, dumped my plate and thanked God that I got by without putting any of that stuff in my mouth. I reported back inside that the food was wonderful.

"Once the Sullivans were doing a concert in Grove Hill, AL with Carl and Pearl Butler. It was Emmett's normal stage demeanor to charge toward the microphone and rake across the banjo as he attacked his break. On this occasion he charged right off the four foot high stage and then ran up the inclined isle to the rear of the auditorium. His running up the isle was for the sake of trying to get his feet back under his body so that he would not fall on his face, break his banjo, etc. He was able to keep himself from falling and this event was the feature of the show that evening.

"The Sullivans have endured hard times and long times over many years in the business. They are truly the "First Family of Bluegrass Gospel Music."

Chapter 15

Rolling Through the '90's
A review from 1990 to the present

MARGIE: One of the highlights of the 90's was our opportunity to record bluegrass gospel for Homeplace Records, a southern gospel label. They let us do it like we wanted to and I thought it turned out really well. Eddie Crook Production Co. of Nashville, TN created the project and I think they did an exceptional job in promoting the project. We got a lot of good recognition and a lot of good air playing time. We really appreciate Eddie and what he's done for bluegrass gospel and the Sullivan Family.

Emmett, Enoch, James Phillips, Joy Deville and I played on the album. It was a good session. Emmett was real sick, but he played great banjo and sang really well. It was the last project he ever did. He passed away on April 10, 1993.

ENOCH: We said earlier, we met and worked with Mr. Bill Monroe back in the early years. We persuaded Mr. Bill to do the first all gospel bluegrass concerts and our friendship built for a period of over 30 years. You just can't imagine the thrill it was when we learned we were going to be inducted into Bill Monroe's Bluegrass Hall of Fame. That was on Sept. 5, 1993. Bill Monroe, the founder and "Father of Bluegrass Music" hand-picked us. We joined the likes of Lester Flatt and Earl Scruggs, Jim and Jesse McReynolds, Mac Wiseman and Ralph and Carter Stanley. The Sullivan Family was the first, and until now, the only gospel group that he picked. The honor of being inducted was a highlight in our lives. You can do everything else, but nothing can top that.

All of these people I've spoken of deserve honors.

They worked for them. They all came up in a way of life that was difficult and put in a lot of long, hard hours and are deserving of any recognition they get. These were happy times, of course, but a lot of hard work. Sometimes we just couldn't see far enough into the future to know that things would work out the way they did. We were all part of a great movement. I don't think there is anyone living who wouldn't think it was a great honor to be a member of the Grand Ole Opry. The honor Mr. Monroe bestowed upon us, is even greater than being a member of the Opry to me. This honor was brought about by the work we did for so long and it is what Mr. Bill founded and set aside for his people.

MARGIE: He created and built bluegrass music. The institution of bluegrass music cannot ever be the same without him. His influence will always be felt because he left such a great contribution. As far as I am concerned, he is one of the greatest men ever born.

In 1994 Mr. Monroe put together some tours. His son, James, came back to work on the road again. For years James left the music to manage his father's office and to oversee the building of the Bluegrass Hall of Fame and other projects for Bill. He was active in the music business but he just didn't tour. When he again formed his band, the Midnight Ramblers, in 1994, we all did a "Father and Son Tour." It was Bill, James, the Sullivan Family, and Gary Brewer and his group from Louisville, KY.

Those were wonderful tours. We got to sit and talk with Mr. Bill a lot and visit on a personal basis. That always means a lot to a person when you have a hero and he takes the time to talk to you.

Bill died Sept. 8, 1996, after a lengthy illness. He was 84 years, 11 months and 25 days old. His 85th birthday would have been on Sept. 13th. After his death everyone helped raise funds to pay for a monument for him because we felt he deserved this special honor. We had a fund-raiser at the Ryman Auditorium in Nashville and it was wonderful for the Sullivan Family to have the pleasure of being a part of it.

It was good to be back at the Old Ryman. We'd been there so many times and there's a personality about the building that you won't find anywhere else in the world.

ENOCH: There's a reason. The Ryman was built as a church. Brother Sam Jones from Georgia came to Nashville to evangelize and he converted Riverboat Captain Tom Ryman, who was a rough and rowdy old cuss. Because of this Ryamn had the auditorium built.

There is a sound there that you can't create any place else on earth on string band instruments. The music sounds different. When you hit the first note you can hear it rebound. It will go around and come back. It's the most wonderful sound I've ever heard.

Alabama Gov. Fob James proclaimed the third week in October as "Sullivan Family Week" in our home state and Oct. 20-21 as "Sullivan Family Days." He pointed out, "The Sullivan Family is the First Family of Bluegrass Gospel Music from the First Capitol of the State of Alabama and the First County in Alabama." On Oct. 10, John Henry Armstrong, chairman of the Washington, AL County Commission issued a proclamation establishing the third week in October as "Sullivan Family Week" in Washington County.

In another honor, Gov. Edwin W. Edwards proclaimed Dec. 31, 1995, as "Margie B. Sullivan Day in Louisiana," recognizing the "First Lady of Bluegrass Gospel Music." The proclamation said she was born

147

Jan. 22, 1933, attended Baskin, LA Elementary, Delhi, LA High School and had written, *Name A Spot In Louisiana*, in honor of her home state.

In 1997 we were privileged to go to Colorado for the first time. It's a wonderful state. That only leaves eight states that we have not worked in: Washington, Oregon, Idaho, North and South Dakota, Hawaii, Alaska, Wyoming and Kansas. We would like to complete that circle before too long. We would like to go back and do some more work overseas. Just wherever the Lord open the doors, that's where we want to go. We feel like He's opened so many door for us and blessed us to go through them and blessed a lot of people thorough our efforts at ministering the gospel.

For the past eight years we have worked at Silver Dollar City near Branson, MO. That's a fun time for us as well as exposing our music to millions of people. Many of our friends meet us there each year. It's a good place to go and we always encourage our family people to go to Silver Dollar City to spend their vacation. You can't find a better place.

In the wintertime we have been doing a lot of fund-raisers for civil groups like the Lions Club, Civitans, Shriners and Masons. We enjoy that kind of work. It gives you a sense of giving back some of what has been given you. It helps communities with their different projects and the people in need.

Some of our fans have noticed a lack of new recordings. We have been working really hard in recording videos. Both the University of Alabama and University of Mississippi have done historical work with us about the foundation of bluegrass music and the preservation of it.

Charlie Waller of Sylvester, GA produced a "Hall

of Fame" video for us. He did a very exclusive job and I've never seen anything to beat it. We've known Charlie since he was a boy. We were instrumental in getting him his first radio job in Waynesboro, MS. He's a fine radio announcer and has his own southern gospel quartet named Palmetto State. They tour and Charlie can do it all.

We did a video for FUGI television out of Japan. It was filmed in Louisville, KY in September 1996. Bill Monroe was on that one as was Ralph Stanley, Gary Brewer, the Sullivan Family and some others.

Lately we did a project for Kentucky Public Television. We did a thirty-minute program and Carl Story's Rambling Mountaineers did another thirty minutes. They filmed it at the Osborne Brothers Homecoming Festival in Hyden, KY. That was our first visit to their festival and the people received us very well. They really loved the gospel. Sonny and Bobby Osborne are fine, good men.

ENOCH: Our band now consists of Marge on guitar, Joy Deville on bass, Eugene Stone who works the guitar and banjo and myself on fiddle. Joy has been with us longer than anybody we've had in the band except Emmett. Eugene's wife Jackie helps with the selling of tapes and records for us. Our son-in-law Dicki Tew has worked and recorded with us off and on and is planning to work more in the near future. He plays the guitar and mandolin and sings. When he's with us, we have four-part harmony, the standard bluegrass quartet. Dicki can sing bass or tenor. He's one of those Ira Louvin-type guys. We look forward to the best in everything. We're all getting a little older but there's one thing we don't have to worry about now - we're not going to die young.

MARGIE: There's no way that we could conclude without saying that we have to thank so many people.

149

The radio and television stations, all the pastors, the gospel singing groups, all the baby-sitters who helped us when the children were young and so many more wonderful people. So many different people made contributions. People in great ranks and small ranks- all have helped.

ENOCH: I want to remember a great family and pastor, the Rev. and Mrs. D. B. Kennon of Jena, LA. He was a great inspiration to me when my dad passed away. Also, Brother Alfred LePrairie of Polkville, MS helped me so much. If they had not held us up in the right way and knew what to do, I doubt we would have tried to carry on. They said, "You must." They spoke to me like my dad would say, "Now son, I know it's hard but you've got to do it. We're going to help you and you've got to."

It makes me sad when I think about the loss of loved ones. Brother D. B. has passed away now, as has every member of his family. Brother Cleveland Kennon was the last one. The first night I ever spent in Louisiana we worked a camp meeting and went to the Rev. Kennon's mother's place out in the country. She didn't have room for us all and she made pallets for us out on the front porch of her old country home. I never will forget waking up to the sound of a whippoorwill. That will always feel like a place like home to me.

So many families like that stood by us. Joy Deville that works the bass for us, her mother and daddy, Mr. and Mrs. Harold Deville and her grandparents, Mr. and Mrs. Blake Deville all of Turkey Creek, LA stood by us, supported and encouraged us. When it seemed to be bogged down and you couldn't go any farther, they just seemed to know where to go. You could even go home, but you couldn't get any rest there. You couldn't get that feeling that you were doing anything worthwhile. It seems like you go and

150

you go and you just get bogged down. You could go to the Devilles and the Hudsons and they'd feed you and give you a place to stay and they'd talk to you in a way that you could leave there renewed. It was just like a blessing from the Lord.

I guess when you bring it down to what it's really all about; there's no money or wealth that compares to the friendship and love of a true friend. They love you at all times whether you're up or down, tired or rested, sick or well.

There couldn't be anything greater than the life that we've lived and the work that we have done with our first goal and our eyes set on Jesus Christ as the guiding light for us to walk by.

Next to that would be the friendship, fellowship and the love of family, and friends that we have known over so many years. It's family, and you know when your day comes, there'll be some of them there to do all they can do.

I remember when my dad passed away. Every Sunday morning we had to pay for our radio broadcast. Maybe there would be a letter waiting at the station from W. W. Hare of Buckatunna, MS. I knew as well as I know my name that if we lacked a dollar in paying for air time, that I didn't have a thing to worry about. Mr. Hare was a mechanic and you could tell his letter by the grease left on the envelope from his rough old mechanic hands, but that dollar was there.

I don't know exactly how to say it, but I guess the smallest or least important part of the Sullivan Family movement thought the fifty years would be me and the Sullivan Family that was on stage. The biggest part of the family was out there, the fans, our friends and our loved ones. Sometimes late at night I'll wake up and a friend will come into my memory just as plain as the day it happened. Time and space won't permit to name all those involved and we pray that nobody will be offended. We pray that everyone will understand that even though we did not call your names that you have been a part of this work and will continue to be. We will never forget so many people or the contributions they have made to help us carry on these fifty years.

There would be some who made contributions that we would never know about, but I know Jesus Christ knows. He's with us all, He's in us all and He's for us all. Let us always put our trust, our faith and our confidence in the future that we will have, whatever it may be, only in Christ.

Chapter 16

The Family and Looking Back And Looking Forward

With Margie Sullivan

Our first child, a son Clyde DeWayne, was born February 11th, 1951. I had gone back to Louisiana before his birth to have him in the hospital and be near my mother. I stayed there three or four weeks after his birth, then went back to Alabama and continued the radio programs. By then we had enlarged our ministry to WJDB in Thomasville, AL. We were there for five years every Sunday with Brother Arthur preaching and Enoch and I always the mainstays with the music. We used whomever could go and help us.

After Wayne's birth we carried him to the radio station because a lot of people wanted to see him. Usually there was someone there to take care of him while I was busy helping with the program. I remember I always had a little pillow and when I took the guitar out of the case, I put him in the case because it was almost like a playpen. He couldn't get out of it. He would lie there and listen to the music and sometime he would cry a little. But, that was my babysitter for the radio broadcast - the guitar case.

Our second son, Hugh McArthur (Mac), was born September 23, 1954. The children were an addition that we enjoyed and the general public enjoyed and always asked us to bring the children. I didn't work a whole lot away from home in those days. I remember I held two jobs when Wayne was little. One was for a year and another for about 18 months. Then there was a span of time that I worked at home and took care of the children and with the group in the gospel work.

153

By 1957 we had two more children Sharon Ann who was born July 22, 1956, and Debra Sue, who was born June 20, 1957.

For several years of our married life we lived in the home of Brother Arthur and Enoch's mother, Miss Florence, who I always lovingly called 'Granny." She was 'Granny,' but like a second mother to me. I was young at the time we married and she taught me so many things. She had a lot of influence on my life. She taught me about cooking, that is the way they cooked things in Alabama, and a lot about love, being a caring person and a good parent. We had a great relationship. I know many people have made mother-in-law jokes. I had a mother-in-law who was good to me, but on the other hand I was good to her. I'll never forget the things she helped me learn. The experiences she had earlier helped her guide me, and helped me be, what I hope was, a good wife and mother to our family.

She took care of our children many times while we were on the road. She had some of her own children that were near the same age as some of ours. When we left, it was a house full of children that she took care of. She always managed to see that they were fed and that they didn't get hurt. She was a good 'overseer.' A lot of the reason the Sullivan Family was able to go on was that she was dedicated to seeing us play our music. She wanted us to sing and play for the Lord. That was her contribution. It was a great one and a very needed one, especially after the children started school. There was no way we could go on the road unless we had someone capable to care for them and see to it that they got to school.

Enoch loved to deer and foxhunt and raise a garden and at that time we had a milk cow. He milked the cow, but when it was necessary I could milk the cow because those little Sullivans really did love milk.

154

One year we cleared a patch of new ground, it must have been an acre, and he decided we needed to grow sweet potatoes. He planted them and I never saw such a harvest in my life. He carried them to work, to all of his friends on the job and we gave them to all the neighbors. I guess it was because it was new ground and the combination of a good climate and a good season.

I had a good friend, Sister Mrs. Willis Hall, whose husband was a minister and they came to our home quite often. We always had such a good time cooking and enjoying food together. She told me one day, "My husband does not like pumpkin pie," and I replied, "Well, why don't we fool him."

"How can you do that?" Sister Hall asked. I said, "I make pumpkin pies and people tell me they can't tell them from sweet potato pie. Let's make pumpkin this time and let's see whether he likes it or not."

We made the pumpkin pies and nobody knew it. It was a special joke between Sister Hall and me. Sure enough, at supper I think Brother Hall ate more than anyone else. Of course, everyone wanted to know why we were giggling and laughing and we just said, "Well, you just filled up on pumpkin pie and you really couldn't tell the difference."

We always had a lot of good times and there were a lot of good couples who had children the same ages as ours. Back in those days, children made their own form of entertainment when they got together to play and they always had a jolly good time. They played softball, basketball, hopscotch, jump rope and many other old time games most kids today have forgotten about. We had a good time on Sunday afternoon or between the time when we went to church.

The whole family always went to church. That was a must at our house. We always carried the children to Sunday school and church. They always liked church and enjoyed the gospel singing. All of them had a little song they sang or they would recite Bible verses and that would thrill us. It was just a part of the way we brought them up.

Enoch was found to have cancer in July 1960 and underwent treatment, but that's covered in another chapter in this book. In the meantime, our last child, Linda Alesa (Lesa), was born on April 1, 1961. She was really a bright light on the horizon for him. He was not able to work or do a lot. Needless to say, he spoiled her rotten. He would drive five miles to get her a pack of gum, if she wanted it. She's still has him wrapped around her finger. Whatever Lisa says is law and gospel with 'Pop,' I'll tell you.

Jack Cardwell of Mobile, AL was the reason the Sullivan Family got to be on television for the very first time in 1958 or 1959. He had what he called *The Friendly Variety Show* and he invited people to be on the program. From our first appearance we became a regular group on the show for a long time. We got lots of response from that.

Later on, because of the exposure on television, we were able to go down to Pensacola, FL about 1963 - 64 to be with the 'Old Gospel Man' himself, Mr. J. G. Whitfield. That opened a lot of doors for us and that's when we first started singing with the southern gospel groups. We met so many of them during those years and enjoyed those friendships. We met the Blackwood Brothers, the Statesmen, the original Carter Family and the original Chuck Wagon Gang. They were all great people and we love them very much. They really encouraged the Sullivan Family when we were young in our work.

Wherever they called, that's where we went. In many states, we met friends, preachers and promoters-people who would call on us. We had to set up the work and that's where I started learning through trial and error how to book the dates and how to group them together. I knew we didn't need to drive to California and then all the way back to Louisiana to make a date, so I learned to coordinate and I also learned that people like to promote. They liked to put news articles in the paper. They called for us to get a picture suitable for the newspaper so they could advertise that we were coming to town.

I'll never forget the first person that made a promotion picture of the Sullivan Family. It was made in the studio in Jackson, AL by Outlaw Studios and we still have that picture. The first picture made after the death of Enoch's dad was of Enoch, Emmett and myself. It was made by a good friend. He took us to a studio in Holly Springs, MS and had the picture made and paid for it. That was Brother J. Frank Wilson, who pastored a church in Pots Camp, MS.

It's hard to separate our private life from our public life, because so much of it is interwoven. We are dedicated to each other and to raising our family right, the best way we knew, and of doing our gospel work, the work the Lord called us to do. When there's a force behind you that's greater than you are, you will do things that ordinary people wouldn't do. You have to make sacrifices. We made so many sacrifices where our children were concerned. Many times we were gone on their birthdays and for their special little events at school. Both of our boys played football, but neither one of us ever got to see either one of the boys play, because we were always gone.

We missed a lot and I know they missed us being there. I learned later in life whatever you lose when they're children is lost forever. You can never got back and regain that, but that is part of the sacrifice of working for the Lord. The one thing I can say to people who feel like they want to do the kind of work that we've done is to be sure that's what your life's work should be. Be sure the Lord has called you to do it, because without His calling I really don't think you will stick in there and do it. I think you have to be called and anointed by the Lord in order to stick with it and make the sacrifices that you have to make. I think that's the most necessary ingredient because if you ever once make that commitment, you never need to go back on it.

You need to stay committed and you need to do it. Be sure you count the cost before you start. In that way, you won't have any regrets. I have to say that I know we've missed a lot of the childrens growing up and we missed a lot of personal pleasure that we would have gained from being home with them. But as I stated earlier, we always made our time with them premium. I know that their lives were not ordinary because how can you make something ordinary out of something that is not ordinary? It was not ordinary in those days to take a band on the road and do full time gospel singing. That's not ordinary. Therefore, the people connected with you cannot have an ordinary life.

With all of its pros and cons, and all the sacrifices, there's not anything that I would change, except maybe to do more. When you look back, you can always see where you could have done a little bit more or done it a little bit better. But as far as an apology for the work we've done in our lives or for leaving the children, I can't apologize for something the Lord called me to do. I can't apologize for one simple reason; I really had no choice in it. He called me to do His work before I was ever married and before I ever had a child. The children were an additional blessing. They still are a great blessing to

158

us. We love our children dearly and the companions they have chosen are close to our hearts. Our 13 grandchildren and our one great grandchild are all so special and we love them so dearly. We hope they understand what Mom and Dad did and why we had to do it. We hope they don't feel bad at us for what we really had no control over.

During the year Enoch was sick, his mother gave us a half-acre of land. We built a little frame house down below her house so we could be close to each other and we continue to live there to this day.

In 1970 the Lord opened the door and blessed us to be able to buy 10 acres of our very own, something we'd never been able to do before. We literally cleared that 10 acres by hand. Later on, another part of that land became available and we bought 10 more acres. We wound up with 69 acres, which is now the Sullivan Family Park. It's not all a park, it's mostly forest. Because we love trees, we hate to see a one of them cut. We love nature and we think those close to nature are close to God. You can go over in the fall and see the leaves change. It's so pretty and it's almost breath taking. Sometimes if you'll be really quiet, a big ole deer will pass right by you, or maybe even stop and look at you before it walks on by. Many times, in the wintertime, in front of the performing stage there will be an ole turkey gobbler and maybe two or three hens with him. It's a fun place and we love it. We thank the Lord for it and wanted to share it with our friends and for that reason we turned it into a park. We felt our friends helped us buy it and they should help us enjoy it.

We still have two bluegrass festivals annually on Mother's Day weekend and the third weekend in October.

Later on, Enoch bought a farm and that's where

his heart is, I think. He had cattle for many years. He's always enjoyed that. It's been kind of a diversion away from the roadwork. It helps him relax to get out and feed the animals and take care of them. He has a natural love for animals. That's not unusual. I know that Mr. Bill Monroe surrounded himself with animals-cattle, horses and dogs. Mr. Bill just loved the old way of life and Enoch's the same way.

Enoch just loves to have a garden and usually raises a lot of our vegetables. I usually put them in the freezer and I make jams and jellies, which we enjoy in the winter. Once in a great while we will butcher one of those beef calves, but most of the time Enoch keeps them to look at and to love. What's really funny is the cattle will hear his ole truck coming and they all get in line behind him and follow to whatever pasture he wants to go to. It amazes me how well they mind and how much they follow the leader. The farm and park involve a lot of our time when we're not on the road.

We're usually on the road 200 days a year. That doesn't include our traveling time. As the horizon broadens we follow any and every door that opens. It carried us to Europe, Canada on several occasions, to Mexico and all over the United States. To date, we have worked in all the states except eight. I hope that before the end we can say we worked all 50 states, as well as all the foreign countries. I can say that wherever we went, we met good people and wherever we went we left friends behind. I guess one of the things that keeps us going back on the road so much is because we try to go back and see everybody again and that's almost impossible anymore. The circle is too big and the miles are too long and the distances are too great.

Sometimes folks will say, "You know how long it's been since you were here?" I'll say, "A year or two." And they'll reply, "No, it's been seven long years since you were here to see us and don't let that happen again."

So, that's the way it is. I guess that's what makes us tick. First of all the Good Lord and second our good friends - the demand from the public to have us come back again and again. One thing I have always been proud of is that if a door opened for us we always lived in a way that we never closed that door behind us. I'm proud to state that so many of the doors have never closed behind us and I appreciate that. I feel like that's a good testimony and that's the way it should be. Always be able to go back where you went and have a good name. A good name is rather to be chosen than riches and a good name will carry you a long, long way.

The blessings of the Lord are beyond comparison to anything else when it comes to working for the Lord. There are no ingredients as important as the spirit and the blessings and the anointing of the Lord upon your work. He's been the other band member all the time. As long as He's there, I want to be there. But if there ever comes a time when He has to depart from the midst of the Sullivan Family, I'd have to say, I'd be ready to go, too.

Chapter 17

A Word From Their Friends

LORN AND KRISTI SCHULTZ, leaders of the Kings Countrymen of Mondovi, WI: The Sullivans are our good friends and we play with them when they come to Wisconsin. They are very family oriented and Christ centered. They are enjoyable and fun to be with. We love their accents and the stories they have to share. We love their humor and laughter. It is fun to sit around the table with them late at night when they are tired and listen to the stories they tell and crack everyone up with their escapades.

J. MAX McKEE of Shelby, NC: They are honest, caring people. I played banjo for them as a fill-in when Emmett was sick. They are great to work for and put on a good show. I got a call at 3 a.m. to meet them for a festival at Cherokee, NC. They got there just in time to tune up and go on stage. I asked Enoch, "What are we going to play?" He was humming it as we made our way to the stage.

RAY DAVIS of Falling Waters, WV: I met them in the early 70's through Joe Stuart, one of their band members. He told me what wonderful people they are. They are always warm and friendly.

They heard of me from radio in Mississippi. A friend of theirs, who was a DJ, played my recording entitled *Orphan Joe*, so they recognized my name and voice. Subsequently, I used them on festivals in Maryland and Delaware. They are always crowd pleasers.

I now work at WAMU, a public radio station in Washington, DC and record tapes and CD's as premiums on our membership drive. A few years back

I asked Margie for permission to include their *Gospel Train* on a train CD. Margie said they were pleased to help in any way possible. They are great people and I feel privileged to call them my friends.

GENE STONE of St. Stephens, AL: They have been like parents to me. I met them in 1978 at Sheridan Church in Louisiana. They are people who mean business with God and want to see souls saved and blessed through their music.

We were in Florida staying at a pastor's home. After church we would go there and eat supper. On this particular night, the pastor and his wife left church before us. When we got to their house the lights were out, but the pastor's car was there. We went in and seated ourselves at the kitchen table. They came in and brought lobster to everyone except Enoch. They placed a cross-eyed crawfish on his plate and we all had a laugh. Then they brought him lobster.

KERRY F. FIGURIED of Springhill, FL: They are the nicest people anyone could ever meet. I played harmonica for them and enjoyed playing for them more than with any other band. They feel more like family. They never embarrassed me when I made a mistake. I feel they are down to earth people who play bluegrass the way it ought to be played. They are fun to be with and are really funny. I love them all and miss the ones who have passed on.

THELMA SMITH of Eight Miles, AL: I have been a friend of the Sullivan Family for about 35 years. They are good Christian people, nice and friendly and the best.

JUDGE JOHN H. ARMSTRONG, Probate Court, Washington County, AL: The Sullivans have been a big asset to Washington County and their home of Saint Stephens; it is fitting that they hail from Alabama's first territorial capital (Old St. Stephens). They lend great credibility to Dixie bluegrass and old-fashion bluegrass gospel music. They are fantastic emissaries of Washington Country and Saint Stephens.

The funniest and most enjoyable story is listening to "ole-down-home-boy" Enoch reciting how the Danish and British enjoyed the family's bluegrass music concerts during their foreign tour some years ago. It was extremely pleasing to hear how the foreigners in Denmark and Great Britain greatly enjoyed this family's music from St. Stephens, AL.

In the spring of 1995, they brought former Louisiana Gov. Jimmie H. Davis, then almost 95, to make an appearance at their spring family festival. They had me introduce him and it was a true delight.

CASEY AND MELISSA COLDWELL of Blountsville, AL: In 1993, Melissa's father, Harold Austin, was traveling with the Sullivan Family. Little did she know that summer would change her life forever.

They were booked at Butch Cook's festival in Casar, NC. Harold and Melissa arrived before the Sullivans and when they arrived there was a new banjo player. He was a 17 year old boy named Casey Coldwell. Margie and Enoch say it was love at first sight.

Melissa and Harold continued traveling with them during the summer as Casey and Melissa grew closer and closer. They truly believe the Lord worked through the Sullivan Family because had it not been for the Sullivans they would not have met. Finally on June 22, 1996 it became official. Even though Margie was not there, she was named maiden of honor.

THE REV. AND MRS. WAYLAND H. VINCENT of Crowley, LA: Some of the first impressions we had of Pentecostal people came from the Sullivan Family, which we met over 20 years ago. They are part of the reason I am living for God today. They are great friends and some of the best people you will ever meet.

AUBREY SULLIVAN of Sumrall, MS: Enoch's dad, Arthur, was my brother and I was one of the Sullivan Family and we are family. They are great people. Enoch and Margie were very supportive when I lost some family members. I will always remember them for that.

BUTCH COOK of Casar, NC: I first met them 20 years ago when Carl Story booked them for a singing at my father's church in North Carolina. Our relationship has grown through the years. They are some very wonderful friends. They are like family. We enjoy them staying with us and singing at our music park. They are some of the finest people I have had the opportunity to meet and know. They are fine Christian people.

BOB AND SUE LANDRUM of Citronelle, AL: We met Enoch and Margie in 1992 and were led to God through them and the Christian way they lived their life. They are good Christian people, not only on the stage, but at home as well. They are true, honest, loving and family oriented. We moved our camper to their park in 1993 and helped them with their festival as much as we could. We traveled with them to many cities. It seems as though our lives are so empty when we do not see or hear from them when they are on the road and we are unable to go with them.

J. G. WHITFIELD of Pensacola, FL: I have used them in concerts that I promote since 1955. They are cooperative and helpful to other aspiring musicians.

They are kind to everyone and live a good, clean Christian life. I like them personally and admire them as professional musicians.

JERRY AND MARIE BRAZWELL of McKenzie, AL: Jerry plays bass for the Workmen Quartet and we have been in concerts with The Sullivans. They are friendly and down-to-earth people. They are easy to work with and enjoyable to talk to.

A funny little story: At a concert in Robertsdale, AL, Gene Stone said, "Come see a duck I have in the car." We went and sure enough he had one that someone had given him.

We have had the Sullivans in our home and have come to love and admire them for the kind of "Christian life" they live. They are very talented people.

CARL JACKSON of Gallatin, TN: I met them about 1970 and worked in their band for about a year and we have been friends ever since. They are good folks.

FRANK (PETE) DEARMAN, Mayor, Town of Millry, AL: I have known the Sullivans personally and worked with them since 1966. They are Christians first, with a devout profession of faith. They are fun loving, joking and trick playing. They care about their fellowman and always provide for their family.

In the way of a funny story, Emmett held a young preacher's hand behind a car seat. The preacher thought it was his girl friend's hand he was holding. To end the joke, Emmett slapped the preacher's hand after he held it for a few miles.

REV. A. M. LAPRAIRIE of Morton, MS: I first met the Sullivan Family in a camp meeting at the Jesus

Only Apostolic Church of God at Urania, LA in 1947. They always preach, sing and play music with truth and sincerity, just as I do, and continue to do so for the past 49 years. They go out of their way to help many churches and pastors who are in need. As far as I am concerned, they are among the best Christians I have ever known.

Chapter 18

A Word From Their Fellow Musicians

The Sullivan Family has many friends and admirers within the music industry. Here is a sampling of what some of their very special friends have to say about them.

CHARLIE LOUVIN of Manchester, TN, a member of the Grand Ole Opry and a friend since the later 1940's when he met them at a show in Mobile, AL: I have known them to be tried and true friends. I've worked with them since my brother, Ira's passing. There are many hundreds of dates I've worked with them and I've enjoyed every one. I hope to live long enough to do that many more times. I have always found Enoch and Margie to be honest, loyal, serious and good entertainers. They have been good for the music world and faithful to God and country.

I still like to recall how Enoch called me and told me he'd had a dream about turning the Louvin Brothers homeplace into a music park. He said he and several friends would come to Henegar, AL and help me do this. I did build a music park there and I still laugh when I think how Enoch suckered me in. He never came up and helped the first day.

In closing, the world would be a better place to live if we had more folks like Enoch and Marge. God bless 'em.

JIMMIE DAVIS, former two-time Louisiana Governor, a member of the Country Music Hall of Fame, who is scheduled to celebrate his 100th Birthday with a concert and party in his hometown of Baton Rouge, LA on Sept. 10, 1999: They are great in every way for the gospel music business. I have found them to be great folks and we sing together occasionally.

JAMES MONROE of Nashville, TN, leader of the Midnight Ramblers and son of the late "Father of Bluegrass Music," Bill Monroe: I first met the Sullivans in the mid-1960's. We have a great relationship, working shows together, having a good time and being friends. I think they are wonderful people. There are many funny stories, mostly between Emmett and me. Emmett would pull pranks on me and when they came to Bean Blossom, IN I would return the favor. We have a great time. I have appreciated the Sullivan Family, Enoch and Margie, and their friendship and I am sure it will continue.

MARTY STUART, a member of the Grand Ole Opry, Nashville, TN: I spent one summer working with the Sullivan Family out of Alabama. The first album I was on was a Sullivan Family "live" album. In August 1972, I moved to Nashville with Roland White, who was playing mandolin for Lester Flatt. Roland invited me to a bluegrass festival in Delaware where I met Lester. I was playing in the back of the bus with Roland when Lester came back, heard me playing, snickered at me and went to bed. He later asked me if I wanted a job working with him playing guitar. I was 13 at the time and he worked it out with my parents.

JOEL AND LA BREESKA HEMPHILL, a gospel music team from Nashville, TN: We are happy to call Enoch and Margie our dear friends since 1956. They are very talented people and very loving and generous people. Margie is one of our all-time favorite female singers and Enoch has a great sense of humor.

When we made our first album in 1966 they booked a string of church concerts for us in Alabama. Though the offerings were small, they shared them with us and helped us get started.

In the later 1950's and early '60's (our favorite years), we were around the Sullivans quite a bit and learned much from them. Enoch taught Joel to be a master of ceremonies. We love these people very much and feel a great sense of gratitude to them.

BETTY JEAN ROBINSON of Franklin, TN, gospel singer: Not only are Enoch and Margie very talented, but they are real and "down to earth folks." I had some of the most precious times singing with them on the same shows. Enoch is a wonderful "Southern Gentleman" and a great musician and Margie is a lady of conviction and anointing and a beautiful lady. They have never moved away from their roots in bluegrass gospel music.

I remember one time we were singing in a church in Louisiana and the electricity went off. I was using sound tracks, so I had to stop. Enoch and Margie just kept right on "pickin,' fiddlin' and singing." Everyone was in total darkness, but was being richly blessed.

LILLIMAE WHITAKER AND THE DIXIE GOSPELAIRS QUARTET OF Kenton, OH: I have known the Sullivans since 1974 and they are very sincere, very dedicated. When Enoch stops in our home to visit, he starts telling big stories and big tales and won't go to bed until the wee hours. He has us all laughing at some of his escapades. He likes nothing better than ham, biscuits and gravy for breakfast.

WALTER BAILES of Gatlinburg, TN, a member of the famous Bailes Brothers singing act on the Grand Ole Opry and Louisiana Hayride in the 1930's through the early 1950's: I first met them in the summer of 1959 in Mobile, AL. I produced the first five albums they made on Loyal Records and made several appearances with them. They are very sincere about the gospel singing and work they are doing and I do not believe you will find better folks or folks who are more dedicated to their work.

When I first met them, Enoch had just had surgery for cancer and the doctors had given him about five years to live. I prayed with them and encouraged them to believe in Jesus. I'm sure others did too. Here it is, 39 years later, and he is still here, blessing folks with his fine talent.

HAROLD AUSTIN of Dunnville, KY heads up the First National Bluegrass Band, worked with the legendary Carl Story and has performed with Bill Monroe: I have found the Sullivan Family to be good Christian people who sing good gospel music. I remember one time when I was working with Carl Story in Lake Charles, LA we had a big shrimp dinner at John Stuart's home with the Areno Boys and Marty Stuart and finished it up with blackberry pie. Boy, what a day we had.

CHARLIE WALLER of Sylvester, GA bluegrass musician: I met the Sullivans in 1955 when they came to our church in Waynesboro, MS. I was seven years old and helped them carry in their PA system. I dragged the microphone and stand down the aisle. A few years ago the Sullivans gave me that old microphone for my collection. First of all, they are my friends, but I am also proud that I produced their first video and also their latest "Hall of Fame" video. I find them to be common, hard-working people. They are very particular about their music. Of course, this is what has sustained them throughout the years, along with Margie's business sense. Enoch thinks there is only one way to play an instrument "right."

It was about 1980 and the Sullivans were in Georgia working a date. We finished the program and Emmett and "Little Joe" were riding with me. We stopped at a local convenience store to get a snack. Enoch pulled in by the pumps to get gas. As we started inside, Enoch gave me a ten-dollar bill to pay for his gas. I stuck it in my shirt pocket as we walked inside. After we picked up our items, we started to the checkout line, which was long. Emmett, "Little Joe" and I were waiting our turn. The lady at the cash register greeted us, added up our total, I paid her and we left. We pulled onto the main road with Enoch and the rest behind me. In a short while I noticed that Enoch was trailing way behind me, so I slowed down and realized he had pulled off the road. I pulled the motor home over and waited. In a couple of minutes I saw blue lights coming. The cop pulled up behind me, walked to the motor home and asked if I knew Mr. Sullivan. I said I did and the cop said, "Well, he said you were suppose to pay for his gas back at that store." That was the first time I thought about it since Enoch gave me the money. I said to the officer, "Yes sir, I have his ten dollars right here in my shirt pocket." Enoch was the most put out man in America. Emmett and "Little Joe" laughed for three days.

RON TAYLOR, a musician from Red Level, AL: The Sullivan Family is charismatic and electrifying both on and off stage. The thing I most admire is their keen understanding of our culture and their desire to preserve it. I am their admirer and friend.

One time Hee-Haw's Charlie McCoy and I were playing the Sullivan's Bluegrass Festival. The rains came and soaked everyone, but did not one bit dampen the spirit of the Sullivans. In my self-penned autobiography, *I Can't Believe I'm Telling This*, I deleted a chapter on the Sullivans. I'm saving it for my next book.

EDDIE PILGRIM, head of the Pilgrim Family singing group from Edinburg, MS: I first met them in 1986 at a church where I was the pastor in Mississippi.

173

They are some of the most committed to the Lord people that I know. They are willing to do whatever to minister and they always give a glowing witness for the grace and goodness of God.

During a long and tiring trip, Enoch was driving while Margie and Joy were giving directions. Of course, there was at times conflicting information and "back and forth" discussions, which finally ended in laughter when Enoch told his navigators to "just hush."

A few years after meeting the Sullivans, I formed my own bluegrass gospel group. They were a tremendous help to us in getting started in the music ministry. They are very encouraging and supportive and we can never put into words what they mean to us.

Chapter 19

Old Friends Remember

Mrs. Augustine R. Kennon, who lives in Trout, LA has been the best of friends with the Sullivan Family for many years. Below are some of her memories.

"I have known the Sullivan Family since 1947 or '48. My husband, the Rev. Darius B. Kennon, was the pastor at a church in Flora, MS. We had an all day service and dinner on the ground. Brother Arthur Sullivan, Enoch, Emmett and some more came over from Alabama.

"Brother Arthur was a preacher and a mighty good one. Along with all the other good preachers and singers, the Sullivans did a mighty fine job. From then on we were with them a lot.

"We stayed in their home and they stayed in our home. My husband was pastor for a good many churches and the Sullivans always came and preached and sang for us. The last time Brother Arthur was with us in church was at Kendrick Ferry Pentecostal Church at Wisner, LA. He preached several nights and then went home. A few days later, we got a phone call telling us he had a heart attack and died. This was really a shock since he was such a young man. We went to the funeral. It sure was a sad day when they buried him. But we knew he was with Jesus.

"Enoch married a mighty fine girl in Sister Margie from Winnsboro, LA. She can preach and sing and play a guitar. They formed their own band and started out working for the Lord. They are still going strong after all these years. They have had some rough times. But they always pull through and keep going. They are some of the best people I know. It hasn't been easy for them at times, but they are still on the road.

"My husband died January 1, 1996. They came and sang at his funeral at the Midway Pentecostal Church in Midway, LA. I don't get to see them much now. But they are some of my best friends. They raised a mighty fine family and at this writing are still playing and singing for the Lord."

The Rev. Tony Carson of Pensacola, FL first met the Sullivan Family at Blue Mountain, MS at a gospel singing 35 years ago. He jokes, "That was when Enoch was skinny, had black hair and a black mustache." The Rev. Carson was a teenager then but says he was forever influenced by the Sullivan's smooth harmony and bluegrass style.

The Rev. Carson stated, "In 1971 I was pastor of a church in southern Indiana, about 40 miles from Bean Blossom, where Bill Monroe held his big bluegrass festival each summer. The Sullivans made our church a regular stop on the way to Bean Blossom. Through the years we become more like family than just friends.

He continued, "In my 32 years of preaching, I believe the Sullivan Family are the most tender-hearted, down-to-earth folks I ever met. Through they've rubbed shoulders with some of the most famous people in the country, they've never once let it go to their head. They've sung in concerts with some of the biggest names in the business; yet their heartbeat is to minister to the little country churches where the common folk are. So dedicated are they to this ministry, that I've never known them to charge a church.

Reaching into his storehouse of fond memories, the Rev. Carson said Emmett was the "clown of the group." He continued, "It was in the summertime, back in the mid-seventies and the Sullivan Family was singing for us in North Vernon, IN. Back then they had a pretty good size band traveling with them, including Carl Jackson and Marty Stuart. So even though they had a bus, some of the boys were staying at our house. We were all sitting around the living room eating, telling stories and listening to music when one of the boys said, 'I think I'll turn in.'"

He continued, "About 15-minutes later he came out of the bedroom fanning, with sweat just pouring off him and said, 'Reckon ya'll could open a window or something in there? I'm about to burn up!' I knew the air conditioning was on and it shouldn't be that hot in there so I went to investigate. Well sure enough, it was like an oven in that room. As it turned out, Emmett went in about 30 minutes earlier and turned the electric baseboard heater up as high as it would go. Nobody liked a good joke as much as Emmett did. We all sure miss him."

"In closing, I'd just like to say that in a day and age when things are changing faster than you can keep up with them, it sure is good to know folks like the Sullivans," the Rev. Carson said. "Their friendly, down-home nature has never changed in all the years I've known them. Martha and I thank Margie and Enoch for letting us be a part of their life. It truly has been *Precious Memories*."

The Rev. and Mrs. Johnny D. Reid of Apopka, FL are other long-time friends of the Sullivans. He is pastor of The Gospel Stable Church. They have had what they term "a wonderfully fulfilling" relationship with the Sullivans for 25 years. Dr. Reid recalled they first met them at a "Fast Convention" at the Rev. R. L. Thorn's church, The True Temple of God, in Apopka.

He continued, "After the Sullivans finished their singing, I went to purchase tapes and records from

Sister Margie. In the course of our conversation, she learned we raised indoor foliage and asked if we had orange trees. Of course, we didn't but we knew where to get one for her. At this writing, I believe she still has that tree."

"Each time the Sullivans were in the Central Florida area we made it a practice to see and hear them," Dr. Reid continued. "After the Rev. and Mrs. Thorn passed away, we started having the Sullivans at our church. They've held many singings at our church and our home was their 'home away from home,' as Sister Margie so warmly states. We love having them in our home and church. They seem like family."

"We've had many funny things occur during their visits," Mrs. Reid stated, "but one stands out in my mind. Rev. Reid wanted to have lobster for dinner one evening and knowing how well Brother Enoch enjoyed crawfish; he purchased several large lobsters and a few crawfish. When everyone sat down at the table, all had a big lobster, except Brother Enoch. There, on his plate, was a little crawfish. The look on his face, as he looked at the other plates and then back to his, was so hilarious. We all had a big laugh at his expense."

Brother Reid related, "Over the years the Sullivans have truly been wonderful friends and made many lives brighter with their testimony and songs. At the time of the loss of our youngest son, his wife and their two younger children, the Sullivans were there. They held a benefit singing at our church and turned the money over to be used for whatever needs the two surviving sons had."

The Reids state, "They've had many different musicians traveling with them over the years, including family members and friends. They've all left a wonderful impression on those of us who have been privileged to meet them. Their present bass fiddle player, Sister Joy Deville, has made beautiful impressions in the hearts of the young folks as well as the older folks. She is a 'joy' to know. We have so many fond memories of this wonderful bluegrass group."

"Brother Enoch and Sister Margie have helped with the milking at our home and any other chore they could," Mrs. Reid states. "Sister Margie is a wonderful cook and housekeeper, in spite of all the traveling she does and is always the perfect hostess. She's determined to help in the kitchen when she's here, but she doesn't let me do much when I'm visiting her."

In concluding, the Reids said, "Their music concerts are like church services. Brother Enoch always has much to say about his travels, his acquaintances (some very famous) and most of all, his Savior. Sister Margie would have been a marvelous preacher, but her testimony has blessed as many folks as some preachers' sermons. She is a wonderful, Christian lady and her music tells of her love of her Savior, as well as does Brother Enoch's."

Chapter 20

The Chairman Speaks

Fred L. Huggins serves as Chairman of the Board of the First United Security Bank in Jackson, AL. He has known the Sullivans since January 1956 and has an opinion that they did as much to help Bill Monroe, the "Father of Bluegrass Music," as he later did to help them.

"Bill Monroe came to the community house in Jackson in 1963," Huggins recalls, "and did not even draw enough of a crowd to open the show. I personally saw him about 8:30 that night in the parking lot of a little drive-in café, drinking a coke and eating a hamburger."

He continues, "Shortly after that, the Sullivan Family took him under their wings and on the road to Mississippi and Louisiana. Monroe had been very popular in the 1940's and 50's, but after Elvis Presley swept the nation, it was down-hill for him for awhile."

"When he started playing show dates with the Sullivans, things began to get better for Monroe," Huggins evaluated. "Finally in the mid to late 1960's, the folk music revival and the idea of music festivals lifted Monroe to legendary status. But it was the Sullivans who picked him up and put him back on the road to glory. That's the kind of people the Sullivans are and I'm mighty proud they are my friends."

Huggins was a radio announcer at WPBB when he first met the musical troubadours and then later the manager of WPBB in Jackson, AL. When he became Judge of the Probate Court of Clarke County, AL he served as master of ceremonies at programs where they performed.

Huggins recalled, "I first heard of the Rev. Arthur Sullivan, it seems to me, in the mid to late 1940's. 'He's gonna preach on the street corner in front of S. E. Roberts' store,' my uncle, Gladys Brown, said. 'And I want to go hear him.'

"The Rev. Sullivan had that kind of effect on people who heard him preach. He was an old-fashioned holiness preacher. But no one doubted his sincerity, dedication to the ministry and his ability to sing a southern gospel song. There were songs like A *Beautiful Life* and *I Can Tell You The Time*, sung in a style that later became know as bluegrass gospel.

"He was the kind of man that the great Dolly Parton later described as an *Old Time Preacher Man* in a song she sang by the same title, that became a hit for her in the 1970's.

"When I first heard the Sullivan Family, the group was composed of Arthur Sullivan on mandolin, his brother, Aubrey on flat top Gibson guitar and Arthur's son, Enoch on fiddle.

"Later on, after Enoch married Margie, the group got it's girl singer, and a little later, Emmett, Arthur's oldest son, came into the group on the banjo. Emmett could play the three finger Earl Scruggs' style, and was the best gospel bluegrass banjo player I ever heard.

"With the addition of Emmett and Margie to the band, one of the nation's best ever bluegrass gospel groups was set. When Arthur died in the pulpit at one of his churches with a heart attack, Enoch took over the band. The rest, as they say, is history.

"One of the best things I can say about the

Sullivan Family is that they are genuine. There is nothing phony about them. They are real people and wonderful friends.

In summing up the Sullivans, Huggins concluded, "They are very dedicated and loyal people who have a sincere desire to use their music to spread the gospel of Jesus Christ. They have always been careful not to compromise principals about themselves or the gospel bluegrass music they helped form. They are an institution within themselves."

Chapter 21

Banjo Picker Plays with Sullivans on Honeymoon

By Royce Sorensen, Chippewa Falls, WI

In the early 1980's I was playing in a part-time gospel bluegrass group call the Calvary Mountain String Band in west center Wisconsin. While I was out of town one of my partners saw the Sullivan Family for the first time at a local church. He was so impressed by them. In those days an appearance by a top bluegrass group in this area was a monumental event. A few days later I saw them for the first time at a church camp near Rush River. They were traveling by motor coach and the men wore matching suits. Their sound and presentation were indeed wonderful. I remember an array of ten LPs for sale. Through my partner's previous contact with them, they had graciously arranged for us to do a few songs during their break. They were very kind to us.

My next contact came in 1983. My group attended a Gospel Bluegrass Festival hosted by the Sullivans at the KOA Campground in Nashville, TN. There I met Sherry DePolis, a Spooner, WI songwriter and musician who has since worked with the Sullivan Family on many occasions and recorded with them. My musical partners moved out of state in 1984 leaving me without a group. In the fall of '85 I received word that the Sullivan Family was coming for a tour of northern Wisconsin and due to the illness of Emmett, needed a banjo player while they would be there. Sherry passed my name on to them. I was both excited and scared to death. I immediately began pouring over the half dozen Sullivan LP's I had. When the first appearance came at Exeland, WI, I was scared, but

Enoch knew just what to say to put me at ease. He was such a well-seasoned professional he knew just how to coax the best out of a green sideman like me. The rest of the lineup included Margie, Joy Deville and Steve Carpenter. Enoch had trouble remembering and pronouncing my last name-Sorensen, a common Scandinavian name here, but apparently unknown in the South. So he'd call me "Rolls Royce" for the rolls on the banjo. They were so nice to me and I learned so much I considered it the experience of a lifetime.

But there have been other opportunities. I worked for them again in 1989 on another short stint in Wisconsin and again in '90. They invited the current group I am with, The King's Trio, to play at a Bluegrass Gospel Music Festival at the Opryland Park in Nashville in September 1990. The most unique time working for them came in August 1992. My bride, Mary Jo, and I were on our honeymoon. Mary Jo had encouraged me to bring my five-string banjo. After enjoying northeastern Wisconsin and upper Michigan we had planned to attend a bluegrass festival in Ipsylante, MI where the Sullivan Family was scheduled to appear. They arrived without a banjo player and hired me for the weekend. Enoch remarked that I must have a very good and understanding wife for her to let me take a banjo-picking job on our honeymoon!

The Sullivans were also very instrumental in the creation of an annual gospel bluegrass festival near Bruce, WI in 1990, hosted by a long time past friend, Truman Strickland. They have appeared on the majority of them and I have enjoyed spending many hours with them.

There are many things about the Sullivans that impress me. Of course their musicianship is top notch——Enoch's fiddle playing is filled with incredible subtleties and Margie's singing is powerful and heartfelt. I wonder at their ability to carry on through the years, to endure road hardships week after week, year after year and indeed decade after decade. I have seen them travel all night in a mini-van complete with string bass inside and perform the day they arrive, work all week playing large and small crowds, staying in homes and then driving all night to get to the next show. And through it all they take time to talk, minister to and be with people even when they must be nearly exhausted. Music sometimes gets to be just a job to some. This has not happened to the Sullivans. After a long evening concert I have seen Enoch spend leisure time picking a mandolin just for fun. They are always willing to encourage fellow musicians and share their wisdom.

Then there is the matter of humor. I have come to realize telling funny stories is one of Enoch's favorite pastimes and he has a rich repertoire of them.

Chapter 22

Bluegrass Gospel at It's Best

By Robert Cagle, Bethel Springs, TN—1994

"Strings!" To many that means an orchestration of violins, etc. But that's not what I mean. I have reference to a banjo, fiddle, a flat top Martin guitar, a big bull bass fiddle and sometimes a mandolin and dobro. To me these are strings.

And to the Sullivan Family, these have for many years been their strings. Not just metal wires stretched across the face of an instrument of wood but life long strings that tie them to their past and to their future.

How far back do these strings run? Who knows! Because you see, before there was a Sullivan Family Gospel Singing Group there was a Sullivan Family. Arthur Sullivan was a preacher. And was he a preacher! His was old fashion pine thicket seminary and brush arbor graduation. He lived what he preached and he died preaching what he lived.

Their radio show on WRJW in Picayune, MS in December 1949 launched their professional career. This brought them to audiences all across the nation by means of personal concerts, radio and television. They have also reached many fans by means of several singles, extended play albums and long play albums. Member of the group wrote many of the songs they sing.

When there are nine children in the family and you live in the foothills of Washington County, AL, there's not much to do but sing and play music. Arthur played guitar, mandolin and fiddle. He passed that along to son Enoch who plays the same instruments. His mother, Florence, taught him the first song Enoch learned to play. She taught him *Wildwood Flower* on the guitar. Emmett, Enoch's brother, is also well talented, playing banjo, guitar, dobro and bass.

For several years Brother Arthur led the Bluegrass Gospel Group to many church services and in the radio work. They sang from the heart. Many times all they got for it was what they felt in their hearts. But they kept on singing.

On the night of Nov. 23, 1957, the ill hand of fate stopped at their door as Brother Arthur was called to cross over to that land which for so many years he had sung and preached. On this night he preached his last sermon, closed the message, turned from the pulpit and knelt at a bench behind him. He suffered a heart attack that took his life. It seemed the end for everyone.

Yet that was not to be, for God had prepared someone to take the reins of the gospel ministry in song and ride on. Enoch squared his shoulders and stepped in where his dad had walked and the group continued.

During the years of steady growth and monumental success under the leadership of Enoch, the family had several members in the group. For some time it was Enoch, Margie, Emmett and Jerry, Enoch and Emmett's uncle. And from the pen and heart of Jerry came several songs. During the war years of Viet Nam, Jerry penned *Merry Christmas from Viet Nam*, which was recorded by several groups.

Why does a group want to sing bluegrass gospel all those years when other types of music were more popular? Well, why does a Frenchman speak French? Why do you bleed when you're cut? Yes, that's right

190

because it's in you. And that's the way it was and is with the Sullivans. In the days of hard times and small response to their music, they just kept on singing and playing. For you see, it was in them. It all came from their heart. And now, after all those years, bluegrass gospel has arrived.

The popularity of this homespun, down to earth music, has carried them all over the United States and into many foreign countries. In the era of loud, electronic instrumentation and in a time when it seems people may be tiring of this loud, sometimes hard to understand music, they are turning to the basic bluegrass performer and his simple acoustical instruments. Now, that's not to say they are simple to play, but simple and down to earth in style.

And in speaking of simple and down to earth, I think it would be appropriate to say the Sullivans are just a simple down to earth Christian family that loves God and bluegrass music.

In many of the concerts the Sullivans are joined by Joe Stewart a very close friend and longtime member of Bill Monroe's Bluegrass Boys. He has been playing bluegrass since he was 12 years old and that means he has been doing it for 42 years. He plays twin fiddle with Enoch and blesses the hearts of those who hear him when he takes the guitar in hand and sings in his own style songs such as *God Gave Noah The Rainbow Sign* and *Eastern Gate*.

On the night of March 13, 1977 at 10:20, the dark hand of fate again took a strike at the Sullivans. As they were traveling east on Interstate Highway 20 entering Jackson, MS they were involved in a freak accident that almost cost them their lives. Enoch was driving their Ford station wagon and was accompanied by Margie, Emmett and Jerry.

He explains the accident this way: "I was driving in the left lane of the three lanes of eastbound traffic and was separated from the westbound traffic by a grassy median. A young man from Bossier City, LA was traveling west pulling a trailer with a race car on it. Somehow the race car came off the trailer, crossed the grassy median and into my lane of traffic. I locked my brakes and skidded three feet before I hit the race car broadside. The impact demolished both cars."

The Sullivans were hospitalized in Jackson in critical condition. Emmett had two vertebrae busted; and Jerry's scalp was almost severed from his head and took 75 stitches to sew his head.

Enoch had five broken ribs, a crushed chest and a pinched lung, along with several facial cuts and the loss of several teeth. Margie's left leg was broken in four places and several teeth were missing. They were to spend several weeks and even months for some, in the hospital. Margie was in a cast for six months and had to use a walker and crutches for several more months.

It seemed the hand of fate could strike, yet not stop this God fearing, God loving family. Their call was and is to sing and preach the gospel. And the death of a Father and a horrible accident to four would not change their course of ministry. They are still traveling over 150,000 miles a year and are now doing it in a customized bus they can relax and sleep in.

The Sullivans have performed in the presence of several governors, congressmen, senators and many great leaders of our day. Yet when they gather in the little church in rural Alabama that does not even have restroom facilities, they are still the same. They still sing the gut deep, heart felt, soul searching bluegrass gospel which has been a part of them for so long.

Margie is a Pentecostal minister. Even though Enoch transplanted her in the hills of Alabama, he did not take her heart out of Louisiana. It stayed there all the time. It surfaced when Margie was riding the bus and everyone was asleep but her and Richard Alexander, who was driving. The conversation turned to talk about home. As the talk became somewhat sentimental and even a few tears were shed, Margie began to write a song. That day was born a song that was destined to be one of her greatest. It was titled, *Name A Spot In Heaven Louisiana.*

I have known the Sullivan Family for over 18 years and I can truthfully say they are great people. I have watched them climb from obscurity to national fame and have noted they are still the same. They have appeared from the Grand Ole Opry to the Smithsonian Institute in Washington, D. C., yet they are still my kind of people. May I simply close this article by saying, "Watch out at the top, the Sullivans have arrived."

Chapter 23

Commissioner Cherishes Memories of Sullivans

Ms. Virginia A. Rogers of Cottondale, AL serves as Commissioner of the Department of Mental Health and Mental Retardation for the State of Alabama.

"I met the Sullivan Family in the middle 1960's," Ms. Rogers said. "I had been singing southern gospel for many years when our paths met. I started booking talent in churches all over Alabama and eventually extended the booking into other southern states. I knew when I met the Sullivans they were genuine."

She continues, "Since our relationship has developed and grown over the years I cherish the fond memories, the respect and admiration we share. It was my privilege to present them a certificate on behalf of Alabama Gov. Fob James Jr., who recognized their contributions to the ministry of music."

"They continue to be one of my favorite groups," Ms. Rogers relates. "There are many reasons why this is true. They sing from the heart because of the anointing, they never book a date based on the expected crowd or the size of the offering and above all they recognize their source, their strength and their eternity is given to my God.

In conclusion, Ms. Rogers said, "We continue to help each other in bookings and in prayer life. We work together to make the ministry of others, ministries of harmony in relationships in goals and in building God's Kingdom. Because of their faithfulness they deserve all the good things God has in His storehouse."

Chapter 24

Goodwill Ambassadors of Bluegrass Gospel

The following article, by Douglas B. Green, appeared in the October, 1980 issue of BLUEGRASS UNLIMITED. Green has since been a member of the popular singing group, Riders in the Sky.

The Sullivan Family of St. Stephens, AL represents a synthesis of two of the strongest and most vital American musics: gospel and bluegrass. It is a powerful combination, the melding of these two musical styles, and the driving, emotional music of the Sullivan Family is no small part of it's current growth in popularity.

The nucleus of the Sullivan Family begins early in this century, with a logging contractor named J. B. Sullivan and four of his musically oriented children, Arthur, Jerry, Susie and Aubrey.

The group's longtime spokesman, Enoch Sullivan, recalls "My granddad on my dad's side, J. B. Sullivan, was one of the finest drop-thumb banjo players; it was the cleanest sound I'd ever heard. We all used to play a lot of what we called frolic music. We played a lot of dances where you'd go over to somebody's house and take all the furniture out and have an all-night dance. But then my dad was converted when I was very young, and started into church work when I was seven or eight years old, so due to religious beliefs we never played anything but gospel music after that."

Arthur Sullivan's conversion was the result of a near-fatal illness in 1939, and after his recovery he devoted his life to the Pentecostal Church as a full-time preacher and gospel singer. Arthur played mandolin and guitar, and, according to Enoch, "he was a good singer, a hard singer, in that good old-fashioned, hard style. Loud—he sung loud, like Roy Acuff. Loud. He believed in good time, kept good rhythm, and sung real loud so people would enjoy it—and they did!"

To this he added his younger brother, Jerry, on guitar, his son, Enoch, on fiddle (he'd learned from an earlier associate of the family, Bud Hiram Lane), and the trio became more and more popular. The personnel fluctuated during the 1940's, and from time to time included Susie Sullivan, another of Arthur's brothers, J. B., and his wife, and the youngest brother, Aubrey. Though their musical inspiration was varied, Enoch claims the Sullivan Family of that era sounded very much like the Mainer's Mountaineers, a group they admired greatly.

The first major change—or perhaps evolution—in the Sullivan Family sound occurred when young Enoch married Margie Brewster on Dec. 16, 1949, adding a distinct, unique and fervent voice to the Sullivan sound.

Born near Winnsboro, LA Margie grew up in a musical family, and at the age of thirteen began traveling as a singer and guitarist with an evangelist named Helen Chain. There was plenty of music on the radio and in person in those days as well: "There were so many great artist featured on KWKH when I was young, there was Hank Williams, Johnny and Jack and Kitty Wells and the Bailes Brothers... just so many of them, and you could hear them three or four times a week, or see them for 20 or 25 cents at little country schools. Of course, I listened to Bill Monroe on the radio, and Roy Acuff.

"Then, too, Molly O'Day and Kitty Wells and Wilma Lee Cooper had an effect on my style—-I never tried to copy anyone, but you can't help but be influenced. I just loved that mountain style. Of course, back then it was pretty well just called country music, not necessarily bluegrass. But we didn't get to hear of people like the Stanley Brothers until later on. We were in such a rural area and communication was not what it is now."

Though they spent nearly a decade preaching and playing, it was right around this time that marked the beginning of their professional career, for it was then that they obtained a radio program. "That's when we feel we truly became a professional band," says Enoch, "because radio then was the going thing—if you were on radio, you had it made. We started our first radio work on WRJW in Picayune, MS in Dec. 1949 and at that time the group was my dad, myself, Aubrey and Margie. That was the first radio work we did as The Sullivan Family."

In the early 1950s the increasingly popular Sullivan Family Gospel Singers (as they were known then) was joined by Enoch's younger brother Emmett, who graduated from his grandfather's five-string frailing style to three finger Scruggs style playing. He learned to play simply by listening to radio and records. Emmett became a professional bluegrass banjoist before he ever saw one played in that style.

His addition to the group moved them from their semi-string band, semi-gospel quartet sound squarely into the then-emerging field of bluegrass. It was far from a creamy success story, however for although the Sullivans stayed busy, even through the difficult rock and roll era, playing the unusual musical hybrid called bluegrass gospel was sometimes hard work: "When it was created," according to Enoch, "there wasn't much market for it. We had to create a market for it. It was hard to get the work, hard to stay on the road."

Though it might have made more financial sense to opt for a more contemporary gospel-quartet sound, style and image, the Sullivans steadfastly refused to do so: "I often say it was because we don't know how to do anything else, but of course that's really not quite accurate. We just don't put the time in trying to learn anything else. What you do is what you like best, and we love bluegrass music better than anything else, so we've suffered through the hard times with it. If we're going to play at all, we want it to be bluegrass; if we can't, well, we'd probably just be out of it. We just love it and are dedicated to it, and though we could have done other things, this is what we wanted to do. At times it was very hard, but it's all we wanted to do."

Perhaps the hardest time of all came in 1957, when Arthur Sullivan passed away. "We didn't know how we was going to do it, but we had to do it. We figured he'd want us to. So we did, and that's when I stared MC'ing, or fronting the group" said Enoch. "At the time of his death we were rehearsing for our first record—I remember he was in on some of the rehearsals—but he died before we recorded it. Since then the three of us have been the core of the sound, through thick and thin, though we've always tried to have good musicians with us."

And surely one of the Sullivan's claims to fame in bluegrass circles has been the caliber of sidemen they have attracted, a long list containing such notable names as Joe Stuart, Carl Jackson, Marty Stuart and Clyde Baum among many others.

The Sullivan Family pressed on through the tough years and the good ones, building a firm foundation of regional churches happy to have them back on an occasional or regular basis. Though now they play a great many bluegrass festivals, it is this network upon which they still rely for a great many dates. Margie says "It's a wonderful feeling to have been in this work all these years, and be able to go back to places we played when we first started. It means a lot to me. We don't like to close doors behind us, any doors, for either the commercial or the church work. We like to be able to meet friends and keep them."

Their first step outside of this large regional network of churches and radio programs (and later television) was their appearance at Bill Monroe's Bean Blossom festival in 1968. They caused quite a stir there with their fervent, exhortative music and driving bluegrass backup, and the appearance introduced them to an entirely new audience—the mainstream bluegrass festival goer—they had not played to before.

"Playing that festival, and the festivals that followed it," recalls Margie, "definitely broadened our working area. And, of course, the more you get the more the demand is created for you, and we find ourselves getting calls from further and further away—it's a chain reaction sort of thing. We worked in over 21 states last year, and already we've worked in Delaware and Oklahoma and Missouri and Texas, and have several new ones this year we've never done...it just keeps snowballing. In fact, it's at the point, with festivals starting on Mondays and Tuesdays, that a lot of times we'll play two and three different festivals the same week!"

Despite the enjoyable times and the fine music they've made with their stellar band members in the past, their current lineup is doubtless the most satisfying to them, for their bass player, Lisa Sullivan (Enoch and Margie's daughter) represents the fourth generation of performing Sullivans, and the third devoted solely to bluegrass gospel.

Enoch describes the current band in his own meaningful and characteristic way: "We have our youngest daughter Lesa playing the bass—she is eighteen years old. And we have a brother and sister, Joe and Vickie Cook. Joe plays the mandolin with us, and can play all instruments, and Vickie plays the guitar and the five-string banjo. Right now we've got three ladies and three men, and I think it's a great step. Those kids! Vickie's eighteen, and Lesa's eighteen, and Joe is seventeen, and I think it's the greatest sound we ever had. We can present bluegrass gospel so many different ways, and I'm so proud now of our band, and of what people say about it. Mister Bill Monroe told me we brought a lot of people to his festival the last time we played it, but that we have the best group now that we have ever had.

"What makes it good is the variety we can present. We've got several different ways that we feature in each show. If we sing the good old fashioned four-part quartet I usually sing lead, and Emmett sings the bass, and Joe Cook sings the baritone part, and Margie sings tenor, and that makes a good quartet sound. Then, by adding Vickie on some of the songs, she has a high voice, and she can sing above Margie and give us good five-part harmony. Then, of course, Margie and Emmett and I feature the old trio numbers, where Margie sings the lead, and I sing baritone and Emmett sings low baritone. And, too, we switch the parts a lot, of course, if it gets too high for one of us to sing—we'll just move around.

"Then we have the lady trio now that I think is real good, the bluegrass lady trio—people really like that. And of course Margie sings a solo, and Lesa sings a solo, and then Vickie and Joe sing duets which are good...there are a lot of different ways we can feature it, you know. We try to do a good variety show, with twin fiddles and a little lady playing the banjo, which everybody likes.

As for Lesa's appearance with the group, Margie is straightforward and direct; "Oh, that's the thrill of our lives! We always wanted our children to be in it, but although all of them can play, the baby is the only one that seems to want to follow it. It's a real thrill to have her." Interestingly, Emmett's children, though younger, are taking an interest in bluegrass gospel music, and though it may take a few years there may be more fourth-generation musical Sullivans ready to join the family in years to come."

Though Enoch states that they are now in a position, after years of grueling roadwork, to retire should they care to, their dedication to their music remains firm. "We have great plans for our music. When we started out years ago there was no market for this music, and I like to think that maybe we helped create a market for it, a wide-open field for bluegrass gospel.

"We used to worry about how people would receive our bluegrass gospel music, but I never feel bad about going anywhere to sing bluegrass gospel music. We know what we're going to do; we've already been there.

"You know, we go in places where they might not necessarily like bluegrass, but when we leave, we leave fans of bluegrass, not just of the Sullivan Family. I think that if we keep on plugging away, we will be always gaining—you can't keep at it without gaining. You gain friends, you gain fans.

"I would like to think that what we do is being goodwill ambassadors of bluegrass gospel music."

Chapter 25

Picayune, MS, Revisited

The following article, by Ruth Stephens, appeared in the March, 1990 issue of BLUEGRASS UNLIMITED.

On December 16, 1989 the Sullivan Family bluegrass gospel group performed in Picayune. It was a repeat performance celebrating forty years of bluegrass gospel music. The group returned to where it all began in December of 1949—four decades ago. Fans came from across the nation to join in the event.

The years between are road maps marking the progress of bluegrass gospel music. The Sullivan Family travels millions of miles making thousands of personal appearances. (Over 100,000 miles and 300 performances during 1989.) Literally marking miles on a map, they are very instrumental in bringing bluegrass music to the world.

The original group consisted of Margie, Enoch and Emmett Sullivan, plus James Phillips. Later came Joe Cook and his sister, Vicki. During its forty-year career, the Sullivan Family bluegrass gospel group changed as members left to pursue other endeavors. Many formed bands of their own. Ten "spin-offs" have evolved throughout the years.

Often family members, including the Sullivan's own children, join with the family as band members. Many of them are accomplished musicians. Enoch and Margie's youngest daughter, Lesa, played bass for four years with the group. Other former band members are such talents as Joy Deville, Bobby Hathorn, John Paul Cormier, James Cornwell, Steve Carpenter, Dikki Tew,

Joe Stuart and Marty Stuart. Although some of the members of the group changed, the Sullivans continued to excel in the quality of music, improving and growing in popularity. Not only have their performances grown in number and reception, their other interests and work in the field of bluegrass music have also expanded.

Recently the group began publication of their own *Bluegrass Gospel News*. Produced quarterly now, plans are to expand to monthly editions. Circulation has now reached 5,000. Unlike other publication, the Sullivan's paper promotes bluegrass gospel music exclusively. In conjunction with the paper, the Sullivans have organized an association of bluegrass gospel bands. Proving to be a tremendous success, the groups number sixteen bands to date.

The Sullivans have been active in Bluegrass Festivals since their inception as festivals are known today. In 1971 Bill Monroe enticed the Sullivans to join him in sponsoring the Dixie Bluegrass Festival at the Lochwood Park near Chatom, AL. Becoming one of the most popular festivals in the area, it was later moved to the Sullivan's old home place just out of St. Stephens, AL. Each spring and each fall it continues to be one of the biggest and best in the state. Besides the festival at their old home place, the Sullivans host or sponsor two other festivals each year, at Wiggins, MS.

In reminiscing over the past forty years, the Sullivans reflect over some of the worst times and some of the best ones. There are some regrets and many, many joys.

According to Margie Sullivan, the worst part of their work is never being with their families. "We've missed so many birthdays and anniversaries. Of course, there is the stress of long stretches of road yet to cover with not enough time to reach our next engagement."

She hurries on to say that the good by far outweighs the bad. Carrying the Lord's message to the world through music is a privilege that the Sullivans do not take lightly. The personal pleasure of serving their Christ is just "icing on the cake" because they enjoy all aspects of their work.

For three generations and four decades, the Sullivans have devoted their lives to promoting bluegrass gospel music.

Chapter 26

The Sullivan Family Celebrates 40th Anniversary

The following article, by Arlie Metheny, appeared in the March 1990 issue of the BLUEGRASS UNLIMITED

Nineteen hundred and eighty-nine the big year of Margie and Enoch Sullivan, marks their 40th year of entertaining as a bluegrass gospel team. Wherever they perform they do something special to celebrate this milestone in their musical career.

A special poster depicting ten-year segments, highlighting their career was designed and was used in their publicity during 1989. Each ten-year segment highlights certain events and musicians that performed with them during that period. A homecoming was held at their park in St. Stephens, AL during June to commemorate their anniversary.

The Sullivans started playing outdoor bluegrass festivals at Bill Monroe's festival in 1968.

"The early festivals were a lot like camp meetings," Enoch recalls. "It allowed you a chance to come in close contact with the fans. Bluegrass and bluegrass gospel is music of the people, of working people and of God fearing people.

"At first we were a little reluctant to play bluegrass festivals, because those were the days of the hootenannies. Some of those crowds were spilling over into the bluegrass festivals and I wanted the people to know that our music was gospel.

"But Mr. Monroe told us he needed us and I wondered why he needed us, an all-gospel group. He said what I need you for is to let people know that bluegrass music, bluegrass entertainers and musicians are God fearing people. That's why I want to have the Sunday hymn singing.

"At that time they were having some trouble with crowds that would get out of line and he wanted it for the true meaning of the music—-the listening and heartfelt music," Enoch emphasized. "Mr. Monroe said that a band could not truly play bluegrass music unless the musicians had been through hard times.

"I believe he is right and I think the working class people out there can relate to the songs of a spiritual realm. When you sing a gospel song and you sing it with an understanding of what the words mean, then the people out there can relate to it."

When Enoch was about ten years old he started playing music in church with his dad who was a minister.

"My dad was a musician," Margie recalled. "He played the guitar, mostly in church and that is where I learned. I played guitar and sang with him in church.

"Later I traveled with Hazel Chain, a lady evangelist, for several years. That's how I met Enoch. Both groups were in a revival service at Sunflower, AL. We were married about two and one-half years later. Enoch's dad was in evangelistic work and I just joined their band.

"We were involved in revivals; all-day services with preaching, singing, camp meetings and dinner on the ground—-a good old southern way of having fellowship together," Enoch stressed.

Right after their marriage they did their first radio broadcast over WRJW, Picayune, MS December, 1949.

"While we were broadcasting over WRJW we met a disc jockey that later came to our hometown. About six months after we started broadcasting in Picayune a radio station, WPBB opened up in our hometown of Jackson, AL. Enoch's dad talked with the station manager about starting a regular program and when we went to the station we met the same disc jockey we had in Picayune.

"They still did remote broadcasts over radio," Enoch explained.

They broadcast over WPBB every Sunday for seven years. Then another station opened up in Thomasville, AL and they went on it with a furniture store as sponsor. They broadcast five days a week. This schedule meant getting up early in the morning and driving 41 miles to be on the air from 5:45 a.m. to 6 a.m. "They didn't have taping facilities and they wanted us to do the shows live," Margie explained.

The first record the Sullivans helped on was an old 78 that they recorded in a radio station doing the music for another man's vocal.

"Radio was the going thing in those days. You'd announce your personal appearance schedule over the radio and you'd have big, big crowds," Enoch recalled.

"They used to have what they called a county singing convention in Jones County, MS over in Laurel. They'd rope off the streets and bring in different quartets; like the Blackwood Brothers, the Chuck Wagon Gang and Jimmie Davis," Enoch noted.

"I'm proud of those because I got to meet some of the finest gospel singers in the world at those functions. They were outstanding folks and people who took gospel singing to heart.

"You know it is very hard to teach a band or a group how to play bluegrass music. You can teach them the music. You can teach them the words and you can lead them to the microphones. But they have to take the next step. You can't tell them how to do it. For that they have to be inspired," he declares.

"I think Jimmy Martin said it so well," Margie added. "Jimmy said 'If I sing a song about Mother, I sing it about my mother. If I sing a song about Daddy, I sing it about my daddy.' I think when you do it that way, you reach everybody."

"When you go on stage," Enoch said, "you are going to do basically the same songs, but no two programs are alike. I have people come up to me and say, 'I want you to put on another program like you did last night.' But you can't repeat that feeling again. Now you can go through the same songs, but each program is different. Each time I go on the stage I search for inspiration to know which way and how to apply it," he stresses.

They have five children and thirteen grandchildren. "We've raised all of our family working the road," Margie said. "They have been left a lot. We have a fine family and we're very proud of all of them. They are very talented and some of them in their own right would be professional musicians, but they have never chosen to do so. Our youngest daughter played bass for us about four years," she explained.

They are looking forward to many more years in music and they are developing a 69-acre bluegrass park in St. Stephens, where they have two festivals a

212

year. They also produce two festivals a year in Wiggins, MS. They have just opened a park in Louisiana, the Kennon Home Place, just out of Jena, LA.

"That is the first place in Louisiana I performed when I was young," Enoch explains. "The Kennons and Sullivans are old friends. He is a minister and has a 40-acre farm, an old home place. We've had several festivals there and the crowds have been good and it looks like it is going to be a good spot. We produce six festivals in three different locations."

They have gospel singing concerts in their home park and they hope to start having them once a month and have food along with the entertainment.

The Sullivans have been celebrating their 40th anniversary in many ways during the past year.

"Over the years a lot of people have worked to make up the Sullivan Family. Many of the past members of our group have gone into entertainment in their own right in singing and music," Enoch stresses.

The Sullivans usually spend over 300 days on the road each year. "We enjoy what we do and we always want to carry a good band and have musicians who know how to treat people and play good music. We like to keep some young musicians," he concludes.

Performing with them at a recent concert in Russellville, AR was Richard Tew, who plays guitar and bass and sings tenor. Richard is married to their daughter Sharon. Emmett, Enoch's brother, on banjo and Joy DeVille on bass make up the rest of the band. Emmett has played with them on all of their big shows during their anniversary year.

In September 1971, they promoted their first

213

festival in collaboration with Bill Monroe, who was interested in getting bluegrass established in Alabama. The festival, featuring most of the big names in bluegrass was so successful that they added a spring festival (May) three years later. After twelve years they lost the lease on the property they had been using, so they moved it onto 69 acres of land they owned nine miles south of Jackson, AL near the small town of St. Stephens.

St. Stephens is a historical site, it was the Territorial Capitol before Alabama became a state. After Alabama became a state, St. Stephens became the county seat of Washington Country, which was the first county formed in Alabama.

Enoch's grandfathers on both sides of his family were prominent men. His mother's name was Bailey. Both were veterans of the Civil War. The Bailey grandfather was elected county sheriff while he was away fighting for the Confederacy. After his election he was called home to serve as sheriff.

The Sullivans are the first family of bluegrass gospel in Alabama, from the first capitol and from the first county in Alabama. There is a long-standing argument between the Baileys and the Sullivans as to which contributed most to Enoch's talent.

"This is where I was born and raised and I want our festival to continue to be successful. We want the people to continue to enjoy it because it is our old homeplace. Also, the climate is mostly gulf climate which is mild," Enoch explains.

Walter Bailes recalls, "My first meeting with Enoch and Margie Sullivan was in the hot summer of 1959, while I was doing some evangelistic work in Mobile, AL. Brother William Kemp, the pastor, had informed me that he expected the Sullivan Family to visit our service that night. Enoch and Margie came and Brother Kemp introduced us. They didn't sing that night but personally I loved their good spirit and zeal. Margie told me of their trial of faith concerning Enoch's cancer surgery and that the doctors gave him little hope to live longer than five years. I could tell, however, that Margie's faith, while Enoch was of frail health, was in believing the miracle would happen. After all his dad, the Rev. Arthur Sullivan (who is now with Jesus) and who originated the Sullivan Family Bluegrass Gospel Singing Group, had imbedded a deep faith in his family by teaching and preaching and living the Bible before them. God doesn't perform miracles you say? Look at Enoch and see and hear him perform in their gospel singing concerts today and then tell me that! You see the surgery was 30 years ago! A real miracle."

Chapter 27

Sullivans Play Important Role in Bluegrass Gospel Music

"We must remember that Enoch and Margie Sullivan play the important role in beginning and keeping the excellent family singing tradition before the American people," opines E. Linnell Gentry of Murfreesboro, TN, author of *A History and Encyclopedia of Country, Western and Gospel Music,* published in 1961 and again in 1969. "Former and current members of their band could make a country/bluegrass gospel 'Who's Who' and 'Hall of Fame,'" Gentry stated.

The author first met the singing group at a church in Murfreesboro in 1997 and again in 1998 through the sponsorship of Walter Bailes. Gentry had met Bailes as early as 1940 at Radio WJLS in Beckley, WV.

"They are very sincere, personal and professional in appearance, program presentations, and discussions before and after their excellent country/bluegrass music programs," Gentry stated. He affectionately calls Enoch, "the dignified Abraham Lincoln of Bluegrass Gospel Music."

Gentry has the distinction of attending the Grand Ole Opry 250 times since 1951, the WWVA Jamboree 10 times since 1955, the Renfro Valley Barn Dance 20 times since 1956, gospel music programs at least 100 since 1956 and at least 200 country music shows since 1940. He continues, "The Sullivan Family programs I've attended rank as high or higher than all the other programs."

"I became interested in country music by listening to current West Virginia United States Senator Robert C. Byrd, a next door neighbor at Crab Orchard near Beckley, WV," Gentry recalls. "He was our local meat cutter/butcher and fiddler. I accompanied him later when he played on Bill Monroe, Ernest Tubb and other country music shows in or near Beckley. In 1946 I gave out cards that included on them, 'Byrd by name, Byrd by nature, Let's send Byrd to the legislature.' The opposition, retorted, "Byrd by name, Byrd by nature, Let's keep Byrd out of the legislature.' Sen. Byrd has won every political race since 1946."

In summary, Gentry said, "I feel extremely fortunate to have participated in the Sullivan Family programs and sincerely hope they will have many additional years ahead after their 50th Anniversary."

Chapter 28

Sherry DePolis Writes Sullivan Song

Sherry DePolis lives in Spooner, WI and is a musician and also a friend of the Sullivan Family. For this book, Enoch and Margie recorded their memories on tape. They then sent the tapes to Mrs. DePolis who spent hours and hours typing them. She has written the following:

"I met the Sullivan Family in Hayward, WI when I opened a program for them in 1982. I've loved them and their music ever since. They are my dearest friends and my feelings are best described in a song I wrote for them:

> We're kindred spirits in family and faith
>   And the music that we love
> In life on the road there's a purpose we share
>   In the world it's never heard of
> Heart to heart, we've laughed and we've cried
>   You've loved me as one of your own
> Though at times we're miles apart
>   We know we're never alone
>
> There's a special place within my heart
>   where only we can go
> Where precious memories of you come alive
>   when bluegrass music flows

Margie's solid gold. She's like a mother, sister, best friend and mentor all rolled into one. Whenever I feel discouraged, I can always count on her to help me put things into perspective.

Now Enoch, he's Lord of the farm. I was sitting

219

in the swing one morning at their house when he came out to feed the animals. He walked down the steps, and without saying a word, took off his hat and swung his arm down by his side like "Ya'll come." It was the funniest sight I ever saw. The dogs started jumping and barking, cows and horses were running across the field, and from out of nowhere, came chickens of every size and color as fast as they could go.

He's taught me a lot about bluegrass music (or at least tried to.) While I was learning to play the mandolin, he took the time to teach me lead parts to several songs they do. I didn't realize at the time how rare the opportunity was.

While traveling, Margie and Enoch would sometimes reminisce about the early days in the music. I have often wished that I had taped the stories, or written down their contributions to the history of bluegrass gospel music. While this is but a small portion, it has been privilege and honor to be a part of this project, to know and work with the Sullivans, to love them, and call them my friends.

Conclusion

So for 50 years, Margie and Enoch Sullivan have been doing their calling—playing music and spreading the gospel.

They have gone many places without thought to how much money it would take to get them there and back or how much they would take in while there. Theirs is a work of faith. Faith that God would take care of their needs. And He has.

Through the years they have sacrificed to carry their music and their work forward. There has always been a driving force in them that these things had to be done.

Some years ago, Grand Ole Opry star Charlie Louvin was talking about the Christian side of Enoch and Margie and made this statement, "They're so good it scares you to be around them." He meant it as a compliment and it is a great one.

Anyone who has been around the Sullivans know that first and foremost they are Christians. They live the life and it shows. They believe in treating people right. They believe in helping their neighbor. They believe their lives should be a beacon for the Lord. And they are.

Enoch and Margie can look back over these last 50 years and be proud of the many accomplishment they have made. They can be proud of the work, of the music, of the family, of the friends, and of the personal life they have lived.

Without question, they are the "First Family of Bluegrass Gospel Music."

Musicians Who Have Worked With the Sullivan Family

Hilton Taylor (D)
Silas, AL

Bobbye Hathorn
Ellisville, MS

Terrell Booker (D)
Eight Mile, AL

Joe Stuart (D)
Nashville, TN

Carl Jackson
Gallatin, TN

Ronnie Dickerson
Pine Bluff, AR

Richard Phillips (D)
Evergreen, AL

Vicky Cook Wooten
Philadelphia, MS

J.C. Henderson (D)
Harrisonburg, LA

Hob Williams (D)
Mobile, AL

Susie Bryant (D)
St. Stephens, AL

Romeo Sullivan
Hattiesburg, MS

Shawn Seay
Chatom, AL

Dewey Coleman (D)
Frisco City, AL

Dewey Reynolds (D)
Milley, AL

Joe Cook
Harrisonburg, LA

Marty Stewart
Nashville, TN

James Phillips
Jackson, AL

Richard Tew
St. Stephens, AL

Lesa Bailey
Wagarville, AL

Aubrey Sullivan
Sumrall, MS

J.B. Sullivan
Holly Pond, AL

Howard Maples
Pascagoula, MS

Gene Arorek
Jackson, MS

Mac Reid
Raleigh, MS

Darrell Lloyd
Waynesboro, MS

James New
Wendy, KY

Harold Austin
Dunnville, KY

Paul MaHarrey
St. Stephens, AL

Daniel MaHarrey
St. Stephens, AL

Tony MaHarrey
St. Stephens, AL

Richard Alexander
Coushatta, LA

Emmett Sullivan (D)
Leroy, AL

Casey Colwell
Blountsville, AL

Donnie Lott
Keystone Heights, FL

Jim Johnson
Plant City, FL

Kerry F. Figuried
Springville, FL

Eddie Pilgrim
Carthage, MS

Bob Burnham
Seminary, MS

Floyd Jasper
Shreveport, LA

Steve Harper
Minden, LA

Jeremy Pilgrim
Edinburg, MS

Gene Alford
Hornbeck, LA

Gene Stone
Franklinton, LA

Cathy & Chuck White
Baton Rouge, LA

Luke Thompson
Baton Rouge, LA

Lambert Areno (D)
Anacoco, LA

James Cornwell
Melborne, AR

Royce Sorensen
Chippewa Falls, WI

Freddie Clark
Rocky Mt., VA

J. Max McKee
Shelby, N.C.

Carl Shifett
Groesbeck, TX

Randy Lindley
Spring, TX

Marshall Fillingim
Mobile, AL

John Golden
Chattanooga, TX

Michael Bailey
St. Stephens, AL

Gerald Sullivan
Wagarville, AL

Gathel Runnells
Hattiesburg, MS

Greg Edwards
Pollock, LA

Tillman Cox
Butler, AL

Earl Sneed
Nashville, TN

Joy DeVille
Turkey Creek, LA

Clyde DeWayne Sullivan (D)
St. Stephens, AL

Bro. Blackburn
Bogalusa, LA

Winky Hicks
Grove Hill, AL

Travis Reynolds
Frankford, KY

* (D) - Deceased

We are sure this list is only partial. It was never our intent to leave anyone out. We sincerely appreciate any and all who have contributed to our music.

ENOCH SULLIVAN FAMILY

Gibb Sullivan

Enoch's great, great grandfather-Civil War Veteran
(Washington County History, St. Stephens, AL.)

Jim Sullivan

Son of Gibb Sullivan, Enoch's great grandfather

Rev. James Arthur Sullivan

1913-1957 Enoch's father: musician- guitar, mandolin
and fiddle
1914-1988 Enoch's mother: Florence Bailey Sullivan

Enoch Hugh Sullivan

Music career began in 1939: guitar, mandolin and
fiddle

James Buckhanan Sullivan (J.B.)
Enoch's grandfather, drop thumb banjo artist
Enoch's Grandmother: Hattie Knapp Sullivan
Dennis Sullivan (1911)
James Arthur Sullivan (1970)
Ethel Sullivan (Bozeman)
Homer Lee Sullivan (1922)
Elva Sullivan (Powell)
J.B. Sullivan Jr. (1926)
Susie Paulene Sullivan (Bryan)
Jerald D. (Jerry) Sullivan
Aubry Sullivan
(3 infants not named - deceased)

MARGIE BREWSTER SULLIVAN FAMILY

Parents:
Otis Leon Brewster and Ruby Alma Givens, married Jan. 22, 1933
Brothers and Sisters:
CHESTER LEON BREWSTER-married Marie Philips, lives in Haughton, La., two sons, Chester Jr. and Phillip, retired farmer and school bus driver, vet of WWII

J.L.-(only initials until drafted, changed to James Lee)-married Irma Calhoun, two children; one boy, Jerry and one girl, Linda; ran a bulk (gas) plant for Amoco, died at age 50 in 1970.

EARL ELINZA-(named after Dad's father-Henry Elinza), died in 1927 at one year of age from complications during surgery

NELL LEVENIA-first husband-James Smith (airline mechanic in WWII), four children; David, Carol, Betty, and Steve - second husband-Sam Lightsey (died of cancer), one daughter; third husband-Roy Poe (died of cancer). Lives in Thorndale, Texas

CLYDE EVERETT-Korean vet, army career, medic; married Edith Miller, two children; one boy, one girl, deceased

DORIS LUCILLE-died at age seven in 1942

ALEX LEON-married, has twin boys, lives in Modesto, CAL., owns car lot and does drywall contracting

CHARLES RAY-married Eva Fitzgerald, lives in Bastrop, La., has two boys and two girls, owned and operated salvage yard, died of cancer in 1993 at the age 52.

VERNON ALLEN-married Christine Matthews, lives in Bastrop, La., one daughter, Pamela, owns air-conditioning/refrigeration business

JAMES EUGENE-first marriage to a Hogan, one son, divorced; second marriage to Jean Gartman, one son, Mitch, lives in Hemphill, Texas

RUBY NADINE-married Kelly Walters, no children, lives in Leroy, AL., pastor of United Methodist Church in St. Stephens and has a tax service business

CHILDREN OF
ENOCH AND MARGIE SULLIVAN

Clyde Dewayne Sullivan

Clyde was born Feb. 11, 1951 and died Aug. 21, 1989. He married Pauline Johnson. He played guitar and was a wonderful singer. Clyde also wrote some very good gospel music. He served three years in the Marines, went to college, was a millwright, a pipefitter and oil well driller among other things. His widow is a home health nurse and is now married to Cecil Walker. Their children are:

CLYDE DEWAYNE: Clyde is the oldest grandson, born Feb. 21, 1971. He married Cathy Wade and they have no children.

GENERAL GIBEON: He was born March 15, 1977 and named after his two grandfathers. He is not married and is in the marines.

HALEY RUTH: Haley is still in high school. She was born Nov. 20, 1982.

Hugh McArthur Sullivan

Sept. 23, 1954 was the day Hugh was born. His wife is Nelda Grace. He has been singing church music for years and is employed at Olin Chemical Company. Nelda works for an eye doctor. They are parents of four children:

HEATHER: Heather married Barry Walker and is the mother of the only great granddaughter, Kaitland Mariah. She works at United Security Bank. She was born Aug. 25, 1973. Her husband is a computer engineer for McMillan Blodell. Their children are:

231

HEIDI: She finished college in May 1999. She was born Aug. 16, 1977.

HUGH and HEATH: They are twins born March 29, 1982 and are still in high school.

Sharon Ann Sullivan Tew

Sharon and her husband, Richard Tew, have traveled often with the Sullivan Family. He date of birth is July 22, 1956. Richard plays drums with the church band, helps in his dad's business, does construction work and also has his own business. He is good on guitar and a great soloist and harmony singer. Sharon is a secretary and homemaker. They have traveled often with the Sullivan Family. They have one son.

RICHARD TEW: He was born Dec. 2, 1976.

Debe Sue Sullivan Warren

Debe and her husband recently bought property and built a home near St. Stephens, AL. She was born June 20, 1957. Her husband, Mark Warren, is general superintendent for Brown & Root Construction Company. He and Debe travel extensively worldwide. They are parents to two sons:

WAYLON: He was born May 19, 1978 and lives at home and does construction work.

BRANDON: Also lives at home and works in the construction field. His date of birth is Sept. 24, 1979.

Linda Alesa Sullivan Bailey

After graduating high school Linda played bass

fiddle with the Sullivan Family for almost four years before her marriage to Allen Bailey. Her husband is supervisor for Washington County and they have three children:

JAKE and JENNY: They are twins born Oct. 27, 1982 and are still in high school.

JESSE: She was born March 7, 1986 and is living at home and going to school.

The Emmett Sullivan Family

Emmett Austin Sullivan
Born July 23, 1936-Died April 10, 1993
Married Miriam Louise Sullivan on May 8, 1957.
She was born October 30, 1941

Four Children

Janice Rene Sullivan Smith
Born December 24, 1958-Died September 9th, 1989
She was married to Gary Smith
She had one child, Nancy Williams
Born April 18, 1997 by her first marriage and two
other children, Gary Smith born March 20, 1983 and
Bruce born April 20, 1984

David Austin Sullivan
Born September 9, 1962
Married to Sherry Jackson on June 4th, 1981
They have two children: Casey , born March 14, 1983
And Darilyn, born Aug. 10th, 1985

Zina Sullivan Motes
Born June 27, 1964
Married to James Motes on Aug 22, 1983
They have two children: Allen, born Feb. 10, 1984
And Chris, born June 19, 1988

Shelly Sullivan Parnell
Born December 1, 1968
Married to Ray Parnell on Aug 2, 1991
They have two children: Brandi born Aug 11, 1990
(by first marriage to Jeff Overstreet)
And Stephen, born April 25, 1994